START
SOMETHING
THAT
MATTERS

Blake Mycoskie

START
SOMETHING
THAT
MATTERS

SPIEGEL & GRAU TRADE PAPERBACKS

NEW YORK

2012

2012 Spiegel & Grau Trade Paperback Edition

Published in the United States by Spiegel & Grau,
an imprint of The Random House Publishing Group,
a division of Random House, Inc., New York.

SPIEGEL & GRAU and Design is a registered trademark
of Random House, Inc.

Originally published in hardcover in the United States by
Spiegel & Grau, an imprint of The Random House Publishing Group,
a division of Random House, Inc., in 2011.

The photo on page 143 is courtesy of Lauren Garceau.
The photo on page 169 is courtesy of Chelsea Diane Photography.
All other photos are courtesy of the author.

Library of Congress Cataloging-in-Publication Data
Mycoskie, Blake.
Start something that matters / Blake Mycoskie.
p. cm.
ISBN 978-0-8129-8502-3
eISBN 978-0-679-60352-8
1. Marketing—Social aspects.   2. Social entrepreneurship.   I. Title.
HF5414.M93 2011
658.4'08—dc22   2011009768

Printed in the United States of America

www.spiegelandgrau.com

2 4 6 8 9 7 5 3 1

Book design by Susan Turner

To my parents, Mike and Pam Mycoskie

None of this would have been possible without your unconditional love and your never-ending support.

SUCCESS

To laugh often and love much
To win the respect of intelligent people
and the affection of children

To earn the appreciation of honest critics
endure the betrayal of false friends

To appreciate beauty
To find the best in others
To leave the world a bit better
whether by a healthy child,
a garden patch, or a redeemed social condition

To know even one life has breathed easier
because you have lived.
This is to have succeeded.

[Often attributed to Elisabeth-Anne Anderson Stanley]

contents

author's note

Friend,

The reason for this book is simple, I want to share the knowledge we have gained since starting TOMS, and from the amazing group of entrepreneurs and activists I have met along the way whom I have learned so much from. Their stories, as well as mine, are told in this book with the aim of inspiring, entertaining, and challenging you to start something that matters.

In addition to sharing the lessons learned, 50 percent of my proceeds from this book will be used to support others through the Start Something That Matters Fund. It is my dream that this commitment and this book will be a catalyst for others as they try and make a positive impact on the world.

Thank you for joining us in this great adventure.

Carpe diem,
Blake
July 7, 2011
Colorado Mountains

START
SOMETHING
THAT
MATTERS

one

the TOMS story

Be the change you want to see in the world.
—MAHATMA GANDHI

n 2006 I took some time off from work to travel to
Argentina. I was twenty-nine years old and involved in
my fourth entrepreneurial start-up: an online driver-
education program for teens that used only hybrid vehicles
and wove environmental education into our curriculum—
earth-friendly innovations that set us apart from the competition.

We were at a crucial moment in the business's development—revenue was growing, and so were the demands on
our small staff—but I had promised myself a vacation and

wasn't going to back out. For years I've believed that it's critical for my soul to take a vacation, no matter how busy I am. Argentina was one of the countries my sister, Paige, and I had sprinted through in 2002 while we were competing on the CBS reality program *The Amazing Race*. (As fate would have it, after thirty-one days of racing around the world, we lost the million-dollar prize by just four minutes; it's still one of the greatest disappointments of my life.)

When I returned to Argentina, my main mission was to lose myself in its culture. I spent my days learning the national dance (the tango), playing the national sport (polo), and, of course, drinking the national wine (Malbec).

I also got used to wearing the national shoe: the *alpargata*, a soft, casual canvas shoe worn by almost everyone in the country, from polo players to farmers to students. I saw this incredibly versatile shoe everywhere: in the cities, on the farms, in the nightclubs. An idea began to form in the back of my mind: Maybe the *alpargata* would have some market appeal in the United States. But as with many half-formed ideas that came to me, I tabled it for the moment. My time in Argentina was supposed to be about fun, not work.

Toward the end of my trip, I met an American woman in a café who was volunteering with a small group of people on a shoe drive—a new concept to me. She explained that many kids lacked shoes, even in relatively well-developed countries like Argentina, an absence that didn't just complicate every aspect of their lives but also exposed them to a wide range of diseases. Her organization collected shoes from donors and gave them to kids in need—but ironically the donations that supplied the organization were also its Achilles' heel. Their complete dependence on donations meant that they had little control over their supply of shoes. And even when donations did come in sufficient quantities, they were often not in the correct sizes, which meant that many of the children were still left barefoot after the shoe drop-offs. It was heartbreaking.

I spent a few days traveling from village to village, and a few more traveling on my own, witnessing the intense pockets of poverty just outside the bustling capital. It dramatically heightened my awareness. Yes, I knew somewhere in the back of my mind that poor children around the world often went barefoot, but now, for the first time, I saw the real effects of being shoeless: the blisters, the sores, the infections—all the result of the children not being able to protect their young feet from the ground.

I wanted to do something about it. But what?

My first thought was to start my own shoe-based charity, but instead of soliciting shoe donations, I would ask friends and family to donate money to buy the right type of shoes for these children on a regular basis. But, of course, this arrangement would last only as long as I could find donors; I have a large family and lots of friends, but it wasn't hard to see that my personal contacts would dry up sooner or later. And then what? What would happen to the communities that had begun to rely on me for their new shoes? These kids needed more than occasional shoe donations from strangers—they needed a constant, reliable flow.

Then I began to look for solutions in the world I already knew: business and entrepreneurship. I had spent the previous ten years launching businesses that solved problems creatively, from delivering laundry to college students to starting an all-reality cable-TV channel to teaching teenagers driver education online. An idea hit me: Why not create a *for-profit* business to help provide shoes for these children? Why not come up with a solution that guaranteed a constant flow of shoes, rather than being dependent on kind people making donations? In other words, maybe the solution was in entrepreneurship, not charity.

I felt excited and energized and shared those feelings with Alejo, my Argentinian polo teacher and new friend: "I'm going to start a shoe company that makes a new kind of *alpargata*. And for every pair I sell, I'm going to give a pair of new shoes to a child in need. There will be no percentages and no formulas."

It was a simple concept: Sell a pair of shoes today, give a pair of shoes tomorrow. Something about the idea felt so right, even though I had no experience, or even connections, in the shoe business. I did have one thing that came to me almost immediately: a name for my new company. I called it TOMS. I'd been playing around with the phrase "Shoes for a Better Tomorrow," which eventually became "Tomorrow's Shoes," then TOMS. (Now you know why my name is Blake but my shoes are TOMS. It's not about a person. It's about a promise—a better tomorrow.)

I asked Alejo if he would join the mission, because I trusted him implicitly and, of course, I would need a translator. Alejo jumped at the opportunity to help his people, and suddenly we were a team: Alejo, the polo teacher, and me, the shoe entrepreneur who didn't know shoes and didn't speak Spanish.

I've been keeping a journal since I was a teenager. Here's a sketch that I drew in the earliest days of TOMS.

We began working out of Alejo's family barn, when we weren't off meeting local shoemakers in hopes of finding someone who would work with us. We described to them precisely what we wanted: a shoe like the *alpargata*, made for the American market. It would be more comfortable and durable than the Argentine version, but also more fun and stylish, for the fashion-conscious American consumer. I was convinced that a shoe that had been so successful in Argentina for more than a century would be welcomed in the United States and was surprised that no one had thought of bringing this shoe overseas before.

Most of the shoemakers called us *loco* and refused to

work with us, for the hard-to-argue-with reason that we had very little idea of what we were talking about. But finally we found someone crazy enough to believe: a local shoemaker. For the next few weeks, Alejo and I traveled hours over unpaved and pothole-riddled roads to get to his "factory"— a room no bigger than the average American garage, with a few old machines and limited materials.

Each day ended with a long discussion about the right way to create our *alpargata*. For instance, I was afraid it wouldn't sell in the traditional *alpargata* colors of navy, black, red, and tan, so I insisted we create prints for the shoes, including stripes, plaids, and a camouflage pattern. (Our bestselling colors today? Navy, black, red, and tan. Live and learn.) The shoemaker couldn't understand this—nor could he figure out why we wanted to add a leather insole and an improved rubber sole to the traditional Argentine design.

I simply asked him to trust me. Soon we started collaborating with some other artisans, all working out of dusty rooms outfitted with one or two old machines for stitching the fabric, and surrounded by roosters, burros, and iguanas. These people had been making the same shoes the same way for generations, so they looked at my designs—and me—with understandable suspicion.

We then decided to test the durability of the outsole material we were using. I would put on our prototypes and drag my feet along the concrete streets of Buenos Aires with Alejo walking beside me. People would stop and stare; I looked like a crazy person. One night I was even stopped by a policeman who thought I was drunk, but Alejo explained that I was just a "little weird," and the officer let me be. Through this unorthodox process, we were able to discover which materials lasted longest.

Alejo and I worked with those artisans to get 250 samples made, and these I stuffed into three duffel bags to bring back to America. I said good-bye to Alejo, who by now had become a close friend: No matter how furiously we argued, and we did argue, each evening would end with an agreement to disagree, and each morning we'd resume our work. In fact, his entire family had stood by me, even though none of us had any idea what would happen next.

S oon I was back in Los Angeles with my duffel bags of modified *alpargatas*. Now I had to figure out what to do with them. I still didn't know anything about fashion, or retail, or shoes, or anything relating to the footwear business. I had what I thought was a great product, but how could I get people to actually pay money for it? So I asked some of my best female friends to dinner and told them the story: my trip to Argentina, the shoe drive, and, finally, my idea for TOMS. Then I showed them the goods and grilled them: Who do you think the market is for the shoes? Where should I sell them? How much should we charge? Do *you* like them?

Luckily, my friends loved the story, loved the concept of TOMS, and loved the shoes. They also gave me a list of stores they thought might be interested in selling my product. Best, they all left my apartment that night wearing pairs they'd insisted on buying from me. A good sign—and a good lesson: You don't always need to talk with experts; sometimes the consumer, who just might be a friend or acquaintance, is your best consultant.

By then I had gone back to working at my current company, the driver-education business, so I didn't have a great deal of time to devote to hawking shoes. At first I thought it wouldn't matter and that I could get everything done via email and phone calls in my spare time.

That idea got me nowhere. One of the first of many important lessons I learned along the way: No matter how convenient it is for us to reach out to people remotely, sometimes the most important task is to show up in person.

So one day I packed up some shoes in my duffel bag and went to American Rag, one of the top stores on the list my friends had compiled, and asked for the shoe buyer. The woman behind the counter told me that I was in luck, because on this particular day the buyer happened to be at the store. And it turned out that she had time to see me. I went in and told her the TOMS story.

Every month this woman saw, and judged, more shoes than you can imagine—certainly more shoes than American Rag could ever possibly stock. But from the beginning, she realized that TOMS was more than just a shoe. It was a story. And the buyer loved the story as much as the shoe—and knew she could sell both of them.

TOMS now had a retail customer.

Another big break followed soon afterward. Booth Moore, the fashion writer for the *Los Angeles Times*, heard about our story, loved it—and the shoes—and interviewed me and wrote an article.

One Saturday morning not long after, I woke up to see my BlackBerry spinning around on a table like it was possessed by demons. I had set the TOMS website to email me every time we received an order, which at the time had been about once or twice a day. Now my phone was vibrating uncontrollably, so much so that, just as suddenly, the battery died. I had no idea what was wrong, so I left it on the table and went out to meet some friends for brunch.

Once I arrived at the restaurant, I saw the front page of the *Los Angeles Times*'s calendar section: It was Booth Moore's story. TOMS was headlines! And that's why my BlackBerry had been spinning so crazily: It turned out we already had 900 orders on the website. By the end of the day, we'd received 2,200.

That was the good news. The bad news was that we had only about 160 pairs of shoes left sitting in my apartment. On the website we had promised everyone four-day delivery. What could we do?

Craigslist to the rescue. I quickly wrote up and posted an ad for interns and by the next morning had received a slew of responses, out of which I selected three excellent candidates, who began working with me immediately. One of them, Jonathan, a young man with a Mohawk haircut, spent his time calling or emailing the people who had ordered shoes to let them know their orders weren't coming anytime soon, because we didn't have any inventory—in fact, they might have to wait as long as eight weeks before we had more. And yet only one person out of those 2,200 initial orders canceled, and that was because she was leaving for a semester abroad. (Jonathan, by the way, is still with TOMS, working on our global logistics—and he still has the Mohawk.)

Now I had to return to Argentina to make more shoes. I met with Alejo and the local shoemaker, and we immediately set out to manufacture 4,000 new pairs. We still had to convince the shoemakers to construct our design; we had to find suppliers willing to sell us the relatively small amounts of fabric needed to fulfill the orders; and, because no one person or outfit could construct the entire shoe from start to finish, we had to drive all over the greater Buenos Aires area ferrying fabrics to stitchers, unfinished shoes to shoe-

The one and only Alejo Nitti. Perhaps the only polo player turned accountant turned shoemaker that you'll ever meet.

makers, and so on. That meant spending half the day on the very busy streets of the city in our car, driving like madmen. Alejo, who was used to it, was talking on two cellphones at once while weaving in and out of traffic as I gripped the seat, white-knuckled. I was scared out of my mind. Not even running a driver-ed course in America could prepare me for this.

In the meantime, back home, publicity kept growing as the *Los Angeles Times* article sparked more coverage. The next big hit came when *Vogue* magazine decided to do a spread on TOMS, although I doubt they knew our company consisted of three interns and me working out of my apartment. In the magazine, our forty-dollar canvas flats were being featured next to Manolo Blahnik stilettos that sold for ten times as much. After *Vogue*, other magazines, such as *Time*, *People*, *O*, *Elle*, and even *Teen Vogue*, wrote us up.

Meanwhile, our retail customer base was expanding beyond the trendy Los Angeles stores to include national powerhouses such as Nordstrom, Whole Foods, and Urban Outfitters. Soon, celebrities like Keira Knightley, Scarlett Johansson, and Tobey Maguire were spotted around town wearing TOMS. Step by step, our product was making its way across the country, and our story began to spread.

We ended up selling 10,000 pairs of shoes that first summer—all out of my Venice apartment, a fact we had to hide from my landlady because I wasn't at all certain that my lease allowed for running a shoe company out of my living room. She was something of an oddball and would occasionally walk into the apartment unannounced. Luckily, her car had a terrible muffler that announced her presence from a block away. Whenever anyone heard that racket, we'd perform an extreme cleanup and all the interns would hide in my bedroom; when she showed up, there was no sign that a full-fledged business was being run out of a residential apartment. Sometimes we'd even hold drills just to make sure we could clean everything up within a few minutes.

'd set 10,000 shoes as the milestone number when we'd go back to Argentina and give away the promised shoes to the children in need. When we hit that number I decided to take my parents, my brother and sister, Jonathan the intern, and several good friends who had been supporting TOMS by spreading the word around Los Angeles.

The studio apartment in Venice where it all began. From left to right: Jonathan, Garett, me, Liza, Hajime, and Allie. This whole crew is still with TOMS today.

Once in Argentina, I rejoined the crew—Alejo and the shoemakers—and together we rented a large sleeper bus with a spacious storage area for our hundreds of containers of shoes. We started in the greater Buenos Aires area and then drove eighteen hours to the northeastern part of the country, going from village to village, some nights sleeping on the bus, other nights renting rooms in small motels. We spent ten days traveling through Argentina, driving from clinic to school to soup kitchen to community center, hand-placing 10,000 pairs of shoes on kids' feet.

The children had been told we were coming, and our local organizers had informed us of the needed shoe sizes. The kids, anticipating a new pair—or their first pair—of shoes were so eager for our arrival that they would start clapping with joy when they spotted the bus rolling into town. I broke down in tears many times. *Oh, my God*, I thought, *this is actually working.* At each stop I was so overcome with emotion that I could barely slip the first pair of shoes on a child without crying with love and happiness. Just nine months ago, this started with a sketch in my journal and now we were about to provide 10,000 pairs of new shoes to children in need. This is when it really hit me that a simple idea could have real impact, and that a pair of shoes could create so much joy.

When distributing the shoes, we tried to be very organized, asking the kids to line up according to their shoe size. If they didn't know it, they could step on a foot-measuring scale drawn on the back of a cardboard box (my mom came up with that idea). But the whole time we were all so overcome with emotion it was almost impossible to be business-like.

I remember one village that looked like a trash dump. Everything was broken down: The houses were barely standing, the streets filled with broken glass and garbage. But the kids were joyful, swarming around us, laughing and playing and thanking us with such sincerity that, once again, we were all overcome with so many emotions. I remember looking at my mom and dad and seeing them in tears, and that just made me cry more, which, when they saw me crying, made them cry again. I'd never really understood the expression "tears of joy" before. Now we all did.

On the facing page is what I wrote in my journal that day.

When I returned from that first Shoe Drop, I was a different person. I also realized that TOMS wasn't going to be just another business for me. It was going to be my life, in the best sense. Each of the four other businesses I'd started were satisfying in different ways, but this one provided me with a sense of fulfillment unlike anything I'd ever felt before. All at once it made a living for me and everyone who worked at TOMS, it brought me closer to the people and places I loved, and it offered me a way to contribute something to people in need. I didn't have to compartmentalize any of my life's ambitions: personal, professional, or philanthropic. They all converged in a single mission.

Once I realized this, I had to tell my partners in my driver-education business that I wanted to be bought out, and they soon obliged me. The sale gave me some capital with which to hire people who really understood the shoe

Oct 16, 06

The 1st school was quite emotional. We lined up in the cafeteria while all the children sitting before us and it was when Alejo addressed the crowd that I realized we were about to fulfill my dream! We were about to embark on the work I knew my life was created for. I broke down like a baby, embracing Alejo, and looking around at all my friends who took time out of their busy schedules to make this possible. That cafeteria will be in my memory forever, and the smiling faces of the children my motivation for years to come.

100% PCW

business. Now, with a few industry veterans on board, we were ready to scale up operations.

Of course, while making plans to ramp up the business, I also started thinking about the next Shoe Drop, and the next, and the one after that. I'd always been determined in my business ventures, hungry to succeed and challenge myself to new levels. But I'm more hungry than ever now, because the work I'm doing isn't only for myself and the TOMS family but also for the millions of children around the world whose feet sorely need shoes.

here is something different in the air these days: I feel it when I talk to business leaders, give speeches at high school and college campuses, and engage in conversation with fellow patrons at coffee shops. People are hungry for success—that's nothing new. What's changed is the definition of that success. Increasingly, the quest for success is not

Putting shoes on children's feet is the heart of what we do at TOMS—here I am with designer and good friend John Whitledge.

the same as the quest for status and money. The definition has broadened to include contributing something to the world and living and working on one's own terms.

When I started TOMS, people thought I was crazy. In particular, longtime veterans of the footwear industry (shoe dogs, as they're called) argued that the model was unsustainable or at least untested—that combining a for-profit company with a social mission would complicate and undermine both. What we've found is that TOMS has succeeded precisely *because* we have created a new model. The giving component of TOMS makes our shoes more than a product. They're part of a story, a mission, and a movement anyone can join.

TOMS is only one example of a new breed of companies that are succeeding at this volatile moment in capitalism. The tremendous growth of TOMS would never have been possible during my parents' generation or even when I was first getting started in business in the not-so-distant past. In this fast-paced and constantly mutating world, it is easier than ever to seize the day, but in order to do so, you must play by a new set of rules—because, increasingly, the tried-and-true tenets of success are just tried, not true.

What you now hold in your hands is a guide to help you and anyone who is interested start something that matters. In this book, I describe some of the counterintuitive principles that have helped TOMS grow from an interesting idea to a company that in five years has given more than a million pairs of shoes to children in need. And I will show how you, too, can create something that will make a difference, whether it's a nonprofit organization, your own social enterprise, a new business you create on the side while still working in the mainstream, or perhaps even a new division of your current company. You will also read the stories of other people who started something that matters and learn their tips on how to make a difference in business and how to make a business out of making a difference. We all come at that goal from different angles, but what all of us have in common is a foundation on at least one, if not all, of six key traits: These six traits form the guidelines I believe everyone should follow to start and sustain something that matters. This book shows you how to apply them.

Together, these six elements offer lessons that will challenge you to look at your business and your life from a different perspective: They teach that having a story may be the most important part of your new venture; that fear can be useful; that having vast resources is not as critical as you might think; that simplicity is a core goal in successful enterprises; that trust is the most important quality you bring to your company; and, finally, that giving may be the best investment you'll ever make.

If you're like me and most of the people I know, you yearn for something more than just business success. You're searching for *meaning*. You want to have the time and freedom to do the things you love and contribute to making the world a better place.

The stories that follow will show that you can earn money, achieve personal fulfillment, and make a positive impact on the world all at the same time. If this sounds like the way you want to do business *and* live your life, this book can help get you started.

find your story

Here's a story I like about two young men, Adam Lowry and Eric Ryan, who had been friends since high school. As young adults, they lived with five other roommates in a San Francisco apartment they described as "the dirtiest in the city." Adam, tall and thin, was a chemical engineer and environmental scientist who once studied climate change. Eric, short and thin, was a marketing professional for brands like Gap and Saturn.

Very occasionally the two *would* attempt to clean their apartment, and when they did, they would puzzle over the scary warnings on the package labels of cleaning products, which seldom even listed the ingredients. Using the products would make their skin burn and eyes water and it made them wonder whether the cleansers were safe at all, for themselves or for the environment. One day the two friends did a Google search on the items to see if other people shared their anxieties. They found that a surprisingly large number of people had been irritated using them.

So they decided that they would make a better product themselves, one that was kinder to both the environment and to the people using it. Given that Adam was temporarily unemployed, and gifted at mixing chemicals, the duo turned their kitchen into a laboratory, cooking up concoctions like mad scientists. Soon the apartment was filled with plastic beer pitchers brimming with mysterious brews and covered with "Do Not Drink!" warnings written on masking tape. They slowly started to develop functional cleaning products from nontoxic ingredients.

Eric then found a nearby business that made cleaning products for other companies and an expert in the field who was willing to work with two inexperienced guys who wanted to create an environmentally friendly alternative.

In 2000 they launched their line under the name "method" (intentionally lowercased), and their first creation was a hand soap that they packaged in a beautiful teardrop container. Eric was skilled at packaging, and from the start method's products were distinguished by excellent design, an important signal to the consumer about the care taken with the production of the contents. But as good as their environmental pitch and design were, Eric and Adam had trouble getting their merchandise into stores. Of course, they were also wildly understaffed, understocked, and underfunded; at one point they had only sixteen dollars left in their bank account.

When they finally did get a local store to carry their brand, they didn't have enough of their shower cleaner on hand to satisfy the store's orders. They had to think quickly: Remembering that they'd given samples to many of their friends, they called them up, hunted them down, collected their house keys, ran to their apartments, gathered whatever cleaner they could find, ran back to their own place, poured the contents into new bottles, and then dashed to the store with the order. They arrived just moments before the customer was ready to give up on them.

But because the two had a compelling story to tell about who they were, why they wanted to create this product line, and how environmentally safe it was, they were eventually able to attract attention from the press, including coverage in *Vogue*, *Time*, and other publications, which caught the attention of store buyers. Along the way, they were also creating a loyal cadre of customers who not only found the product useful but felt connected to a story that moved them and a movement that became part of *their* story.

To keep things simple and transparent, the company also created what they called the Dirty List. If they discover that any commonly used ingredient is unhealthy for homes or for the planet, that ingredient is banished from ever being used by method. For instance, beef fat is commonly used as a softening agent in dryer sheets across the industry, but beef fat is a "dirty" ingredient: Many people would be horrified to know that their clothes get a little softer in the dryer because cattle were slaughtered. Beef fat is banned from method products. Instead, method dryer sheets are embedded with plant-based oilseed. The story of method is also one of their favorite slogans: "People Against Dirty."

Today, method is one of the world's largest eco-friendly cleaning brands, selling its merchandise in national stores including Whole Foods, Target, Costco, Duane Reade, and Staples. It has been featured on the Home Shopping Network, and its liquid hand soap is number three in the category in sales. *Fast Company* magazine ranked method as the sixteenth-most-innovative company in the world; in 2006, *Inc.* magazine ranked it the seventh-fastest-growing company in the United States: Sales rose from less than $90,000 in 2001 to around $100 million in 2010.

Not only that, but Eric and Adam were named PETA's "Persons of the Year" in 2006 and were featured in *Time* magazine's 2006 "Who's Who Eco Guide."

All this happened because Eric and Adam had an idea, a story to tell, and, eventually, a product to sell. From their very first sale, they led with their story—the personal story of two guys worried about the toxicity of the products they cleaned with, and the professional story of a company that approached cleaning in an environmentally friendly way. These stories allowed them to funnel excitement about the brand to consumers, who otherwise don't spend much time thinking about cleansers—and for good reason. Method gave them a reason to make a previously thoughtless decision into a meaningful one.

THE POWER OF STORIES

Stories are the most primitive and purest form of communication. The most enduring and galvanizing ideas and values of our civilization are embedded in our stories, from those of Homer, whose preliterate epic poems united the Greeks' national spirit, and Virgil, whose poems did the same for the Romans, to those told by Jesus, who used parables to teach his disciples. It seems to be in our genetic makeup to capture our best ideas in stories, to enjoy them, to learn from them, and to pass them on to others.

According to renowned storyteller and author Kendall Haven (author of *Super Simple Storytelling*), "Human minds rely on stories and story architecture as the primary road map for understanding, making sense of, remembering, and planning our lives—as well as the countless experiences and narratives we encounter along the way." Smart, future-oriented companies use this ancient impulse in new ways, by telling stories that people can watch on YouTube and share on Facebook.

When you have a memorable story about who you are and what your mission is, your success no longer depends on how experienced you are or how many degrees you have or who you know. A good story transcends boundaries, breaks barriers, and opens doors. It is a key not only to starting a business but also to clarifying your own personal identity and choices.

A story evokes emotion, and emotion forges a connection. This is why the way companies introduce themselves to customers has changed. They can no longer rely on simple, straightforward ad campaigns, the kind portrayed on the television show *Mad Men*. The *Mad Men* style of advertising was effective during an era when there were only three channels on your television. Back then, major brands controlled the conversation by bombarding consumers with pitches such as: *Ford trucks are the toughest; Crest toothpaste makes teeth their whitest; Coca-Cola is the most refreshing soft drink.*

I don't believe those work today. The media are much more fragmented and the attention of consumers more divided.

People are no longer all listening to or watching the same few radio or TV stations each week—they're following their own carefully curated Twitter feeds, commenting on and creating blogs, channel surfing among more than 500 TV stations, watching Hulu on laptops, clicking on YouTube, reading Kindles and Nooks, and surfing on iPads. Sometimes all at the same time.

It may seem counterintuitive, but because so many product claims and consumer opinions are a click away, it's actually more, not less, difficult to base purchasing decisions on this information. Not only is there too much to sift through, but much of it is contradictory: Chevrolet is the best car—or the worst—depending on which you follow. Crest cleans teeth their whitest—or does Colgate? An article on the Web says one thing, but the stream of comments under it says something different.

And unless this information is presented in an emotionally compelling fashion in the first place, you'll probably forget most of it almost immediately. Business consultant Annette Simmons explained this phenomenon: "Facts are neutral until human beings add their own meaning to those facts. People make their decisions based on what the facts mean to them, not on the facts themselves. The meaning they add to facts depends on their current story . . . facts are not terribly useful to influencing others. People don't need new facts—they need a new *story*."

A barrage of facts is simply not as powerful as a simple, well-told story—and science offers proof. In 2009, Carnegie Mellon University researchers compared how our behavior is affected by abstract facts versus a concrete story. The team offered students five dollars to complete a survey about various technological gadgets. Unknown to the students was that the questions had nothing to do with the study. Instead, the research focused on what happened when they got paid for their participation. At the end of the "study," students received five one-dollar bills and one of two letters asking them to donate some of their newly earned money to Save the Children, a well-known international charity.

One of the letters was studded with facts about food shortages in Malawi and statistics correlating severe rainfall deficits with fewer crops. The other told the riveting story of a desperately poor seven-year-old Malawian girl named Rokia.

The students who received the letter filled with statistics contributed an average of $1.14. The students who read the story of Rokia contributed $2.38. That's more than twice as much!

The researchers then gave a third group of people *both* letters—one full of statistics and one with the story of Rokia. These students gave almost a dollar less than the people who saw only the story about Rokia.

Facts are important, but the story matters. Poorly presented facts can even get in the way of the story's impact.

Seth Godin is one of my favorite business gurus and is especially astute in describing the value of storytelling in business: "People just aren't that good at remembering facts," he wrote in his book *Meatball Sundae*. "When people do remember facts, it's almost always in context. Patagonia makes warm coats. So do many other companies, almost all of which sell their coats for less money, do less volume, and turn a lower profit. Is it because Patagonia coats are more beautiful or warmer? Not at all. It's because the company has created (and lives) a story that has less to do with clothing and more to do with the environment. Their mission statement is: Build the best product, cause no unnecessary harm, use business to inspire and implement solutions to the environmental crisis. And the company absolutely adheres to that mission."

Actually, one of the most successful recent uses of story in advertising came about by accident. In the late 1990s, the fast-food company Subway created a new line of healthy sandwiches and, along with it, an advertising campaign centered on an impersonal numbers-based product description: They were introducing seven subs that each contained less than six grams of fat.

Few consumers cared. But then, in 1999, Subway accidentally discovered Jared Fogle, a onetime 425-pound college student who had been diagnosed with edema, a condition that can lead to diabetes, cardiovascular disease, and other severe health problems. Jared, who at the time had a sixty-inch waist, knew he had to lose weight to avoid serious illness; to do that, he started eating what he called "The Subway Diet"—a low-fat sub for lunch and another for dinner.

Three months later, Jared had lost almost one hundred pounds and was on his way to losing more—so much that newspaper and magazine articles began to appear about his counterintuitive diet of sandwiches. A Subway franchise owner read one of these articles and sent it to Subway's ad agency; they in turn tracked down Jared. Some company executives weren't convinced that Jared's story, memorable as it was, would sell sandwiches, so Subway tried a Jared-based advertising campaign in select locations as an experiment. The results were spectacular. Subway eventually rolled out a major national campaign built around the story of Jared.

The seven-under-six campaign had gone nowhere, but the Jared story gave the company an 18 percent increase in sales its first year and another 16 percent the year after that, at a time when other chains were growing at less than half that rate.

STORIES RESONATE MORE THAN FACTS

Frankly, I didn't know this lesson when we started TOMS—but I learned it pretty quickly. In fact, I know the exact moment I realized that TOMS was a story as much as it was a product.

Back in November of 2006, I was checking in to a flight at New York's JFK Airport on my way to Los Angeles. At the time I wasn't wearing my TOMS because I had come directly from the gym, in a rush to catch the plane, and still had on my sneakers. That was very unusual for me— I almost always wear TOMS.

The trip had been difficult. At the time, TOMS was a very young company, and the tough and jaded buyers at the major New York fashion retailers didn't yet understand our mission. I hadn't made one sale in the city that week and was leaving feeling a little deflated.

While I was checking in at the American Airlines automated kiosk, I noticed that the woman next to me was wearing a pair of red TOMS. Now, at this early point in TOMS' history, I still hadn't seen a single person outside of friends, family, and interns wearing our shoes. This was a big moment for me.

Containing my excitement, I said, "I really like your red shoes. What are they?"

It was as if I'd pushed a button on the kiosk; the response was that automatic. The woman's eyes widened, her face came alive, and she said boldly, "TOMS!"

Trying to be cool, I kept watching the ticketing kiosk, but the woman became so excited that she grabbed my shoulder, pulled me away from the machine, and, in an animated voice, told me the TOMS story.

"You don't understand," she said. "When I bought this pair of shoes, they actually gave a pair of shoes to a child in Argentina. And there's this guy who lives in Los Angeles

who went to Argentina on vacation who had this idea—
I think he lives on a boat and he was once on the *Amazing
Race* TV show—and the company is wonderful, and they've
already given away thousands of shoes!"

At this point I was getting embarrassed and knew I had
to tell her who I was—I couldn't walk away from such excitement. So I said, "Actually, I'm Blake. I started TOMS."

She looked me right in the eyes and said, "Why did you
cut your hair?"

This wasn't the question I'd expected. But it turned out
she had seen the YouTube videos we'd created on a TOMS
Shoe Drop—when I had much longer hair, which is why she
didn't recognize me. But it also showed how much attention
the woman paid to the video and to our company.

I gave her a hug and proceeded to my gate. Only when I
was seated on the plane did the magic of what had just happened dawn on me: This woman was passionate about telling the TOMS story to a *complete stranger*. How many other
people had she already spoken to? If she was willing to talk
like this to me, she'd probably told her family and friends as
well. She might even have uploaded a photo of her shoes to
Facebook and shared the YouTube video with her friends.
How many people had she influenced?

I wondered, "What happens when we have ten thousand
or one hundred thousand people wearing TOMS? If they
all tell the story to only three or four others, and then those
people tell the story . . ." Well, you can do the math.

That's when I fully realized the power of our story. And
we've been focused on it ever since.

The story helped us understand another important point. People who tell the TOMS story are more than just our customers, they're our supporters. People who buy TOMS like to talk about their support of our mission rather than simply telling people they bought a nice shoe from some random shoe company. They support the product, and the story, in a way that a casual buyer will never do. Supporters beat customers every time.

But gaining supporters starts with having a story worth supporting. Exxon Mobil can come up with a story if it wants, and if it pays enough PR companies enough money, it can put a positive spin on its business: Still, the focus of Exxon Mobil (or Union Carbide or Philip Morris or Goldman Sachs) will always be on making money above all else, a perfectly defensible capitalist motivation. But no one bypasses a Shell station to go to an Exxon because of the "Exxon story."

Conscious capitalism is about more than simply making money—although it's about that too. It's about creating a successful business that also connects supporters to something that matters to them and that has great impact in the world. As consumers, customers will want your product for the typical reasons—because it works better, because it's fashionable, because the price is competitive, because it offers an innovation—but as supporters they also *believe* in what you're doing; they've bought into your story because it taps into something real, and they want to be a part of it.

This is why the woman at the airport matters. Every

For more than sixty days, I crisscrossed the country in an Airstream trailer telling the TOMS story. This photo was taken outside a Nordstrom parking lot where we camped for the night.

company needs supporters like her. Customers and employees come and go. Supporters are with you for the long haul.

AT&T entered the TOMS story at just the right time: The company played an enormous role in our growth—and in helping tens of thousands of children receive shoes in 2009. The relationship came about through a serendipitous act of storytelling.

FEET FIRST

When we started TOMS, I used to wear one shoe from each of two different pairs wherever I went. On my left foot I'd wear a red one and on my right, a blue one. (Sometimes I'd don a tie-dyed one on the left and a black one on the right.) The point was to make people notice, so that when they asked about my mismatched shoes, I could tell them the TOMS story. It worked: I was able to tell the story so many more times than if I was just wearing a matching pair of TOMS.

In 2008, I had filmed a minute-and-a-half television interview for LXTV, an NBC affiliate, in which I talked about the TOMS story. The segment wound up running on video screens in the backs of 5,000 New York City cabs and was viewed by hundreds of thousands of riders.

One of those taxicab riders happened to be an executive from the ad agency BBDO, which does a lot of work with AT&T. The people at BBDO thought that the TOMS story would be a great fit for an AT&T campaign they were putting together, so they sent an email to info@TOMS.com (our customer-service email account). Once they found out that I actually used AT&T to run my business from overseas, the company asked me to film a commercial. Directed by Oscar nominee Bennett Miller (*Capote*), the shoot took place over a week's stretch, mostly at TOMS headquarters in Santa Monica and on location at a Shoe Drop in Uruguay.

The commercial ran throughout 2009 and was an enormous success, both for AT&T and for TOMS. AT&T benefited from their connection to our story—TOMS gave them an inspiring, human-scale way to connect to people (just as Jared did for Subway in a very different sort of campaign). And TOMS benefited from the exposure of being a part of a global brand's massive ad buy. The lesson: The power of your story isn't just a way to connect to your ultimate consumer but is also a means of making you attractive to potential partners who want to attach themselves to something deeper than buying and selling.

ASSIGNMENT: FIND YOUR STORY

Now think about how to find your own story. Here are some tips to do just that.

THE POWER OF AFFINITY

There's a new vodka called Tito's that is ubiquitous in Texas restaurants because, in a world already full of premium vodkas like Grey Goose, Smirnoff, and Absolut, it's the only one actually *from* Texas. Company founder Bert Butler Beveridge II, aka "Tito," was able to use this distinction to enter the premium-vodka market, which everyone else felt was already overly saturated. Instead of just creating another high-end vodka to compete with the established brands, Bert created a story—the only Texan vodka—and quickly received support from restaurateurs around the state who, out of Texas pride, wanted to help him.

Everyone belongs to some community, whether it's based on your background, your home state, your college, or your favorite sports team. By identifying all the possible communities to which you belong, you may well find an affinity group—and a story—that helps get your business off the ground, secures your dream job, or lets you achieve whatever goal you are pursuing.

Almost everyone has a passion for something, but sometimes we have trouble saying what it is. It's surprisingly easy to lose touch with our true passions—sometimes because we get distracted with everyday living; sometimes simply because in the usual stream of small talk or transactable business, no one ever asks us about our dreams. That's why it's so important that you first find a way to articulate your passion *to yourself.* When you discover what your passion is, you will have found your story as well.

If you're not sure about your passion, here are three questions I sometimes ask people:

- If you did not have to worry about money, what would you do with your time?

- What kind of work would you want to do?

- What cause would you serve?

Once you answer these questions, you'll have a good idea of what your passion is. Take your time—you might need to let the questions sit with you for just a moment before you reconnect to your truest answers. But once you figure out what your passion is, you have the core of your story and the beginning of your project.

The more strongly you feel about what you do, the more likely you are to push yourself to be good at it and find a way to make a success of it. If you organize your life around your passion, you can turn your passion into your story and then turn your story into something bigger—something that matters.

TELLING YOUR STORY TO THE WORLD

Once you figure out your story and begin your project—be it a business, a philanthropic organization, or even a job search—how do you spread it? The most important thing is that you *commit* to telling that story at every opportunity. It's not an incidental part of your business; it has to be a major area of focus—otherwise, you won't spend the time you need to promote and share it.

At TOMS, our story is very simple: We make great shoes and give away a pair to a child in need for every pair we sell. And we recently began using our One for One model to help save and restore sight through the launch of TOMS Eyewear. For every pair of sunglasses or eyewear we sell, TOMS helps give sight to a person in need through medical treatment, prescription glasses, or eye surgeries administered by our amazing eye care partner Seva.

We spend every day thinking about new ways to spread our story. We've done everything from a seventy-day cross-country tour in an Airstream trailer to hosting events at Nordstrom stores to inviting fans and customers to join us on Shoe Drops around the world, and from creating a thirty-five-minute documentary we premiered at the Tribeca Film Festival to developing a TOMS campus department to support high school and college students who want to join the movement.

We are also quick to use ideas that come from our supporters, rather than our own brainstorming. For example, in 2008, students at the TOMS campus club at Pepperdine University organized a barefoot walk on campus to raise awareness of what it feels like not to have shoes. We thought it was a terrific idea, and soon TOMS launched an official company program called One Day Without Shoes (ODWS), which takes place every April. We ask our customers and fans to go barefoot for one day—just as the students at Pepperdine did. ODWS walks have been organized at elementary schools, high schools, college campuses, companies big and small, and hundreds of other places. In 2010, more than 250,000 people around the world participated in ODWS, 1,600 of which were organized through our website. (Please come join us at www.onedaywithoutshoes.com.)

Don't ever think that good ideas will come only from within your organization—sometimes your supporters will think up ideas as good as anything your employees could ever invent.

TOMS never stops thinking of new ways to tell our story, because we believe in it. People outside an organization can sense the difference between a story that is authentic and a story that was fabricated just to make money—but so can people within an organization. So can you, as the leader of your project, whatever it is, and if you doubt your own authenticity, it will sap your passion. But if you genuinely love your story, you will love to share it with others.

H ere are some other tips for spreading your story:

SHARE YOUR STORY
WITH EVERYONE YOU CAN

Make a list of every group to which you have a connection and that could help get it out there. This list might include your social network online (e.g., Facebook friends, Twitter followers), an alumni organization, a weekend sports team, yoga class members, a church congregation, and so on. These are your communities, and they already have a vested interest (even if loosely) in what you are doing with your life.

But don't stop there. Talk up your story anywhere someone is likely to ask you, "So what do you do?" Some of my favorite places to engage in this kind of story-sharing are ski lifts, subways, planes, holiday parties, business networking events, and trade shows. Take the opportunity to let your passion run wild. Again, you'll quickly see if your story is resonating or falling flat—not only are you spreading your story, but you're also finding new ways to refine it.

FIND STORY PARTNERS

Stories don't have to stand alone. If your story resonates with someone else's, find a way to merge the stories, as AT&T did with TOMS.

When you have a story that's larger and more interesting than your product or service—or you—other people and companies will want to incorporate your story into theirs to share in the halo effect. For TOMS, those people and companies included the publisher of *Vogue*, who gave TOMS as a holiday gift to his extraordinary list of contacts (most of whom had not heard of TOMS at the time); Ralph Lauren, who created a line of limited-edition TOMS featuring special prints and patches and sold them in Rugby by Ralph Lauren retail stores across the country; and the high-end clothing store Theory, which featured TOMS on its sixty-foot "Icon Wall" at its flagship Manhattan store and on smaller walls at other locations. Each wall featured the word "GIVE" spelled out in giant capital letters, along with text retelling the TOMS story. Theory did all this with a simple objective: sharing a story they liked with their customers.

CAREFULLY MANAGE YOUR ONLINE STORY

If someone is interested in hiring you, or consulting with you, or joining your business, or even dating you, he or she will go online and Google you. Your Facebook page or your Tumblr or your Flickr feed will appear, and if they're not compelling, if they don't offer opportunities for others to feel a connection to your story, it will be very hard to stand out.

The solution is not to try to scrub the Internet clean

As part of One Day Without Shoes, the TOMS staff and local fans walk barefoot along the Santa Monica Pier. In 2010, more than 250,000 people went barefoot on ODWS.

of your presence. Quite the opposite: You want prospective partners, employers, colleagues (and dates) to find you—your online presence gives you a wonderful way to affirm the impression you make in person. But the key is to make sure that the online persona represents who you really are and is consistent with the themes of your story—and take care that you don't put anything out there that you don't want someone to find. Google doesn't care if your search results embarrass you.

FIND THE INFLUENCE MAKERS
WHO WILL LOVE YOUR STORY

In every niche there are the people Malcolm Gladwell famously labeled "connectors" in his book *The Tipping Point*, the bigmouths who are at the hub of their networks. Make sure to get your story in front of people who are in a position to tell it to others. Sharing your story with a hermit may earn you one new convert; sharing it with someone at the center of a social network will have an exponential effect.

THE SHEEX FACTOR

For many years, Susan Walvius was one of women's college basketball's most successful coaches, working at several schools before taking a job at the University of South Carolina, where in 2002 her team made it to the Elite Eight in the National Collegiate Athletic Association (NCAA) tournament. Michelle Marciniak is a former basketball star who competed in two national championships during her career at the University of Tennessee (and was named Most Valuable Player in the 1996 NCAA Final Four). After a stint with the Women's National Basketball Association, she went on to work with Susan at South Carolina.

Involved in sports for more than two decades, the two women had developed an expertise in sportswear fabrics. One day Michelle found a new one that she loved and brought it for Susan to examine. Susan thought it was terrific and said, "I'd love to have bedsheets made of this stuff."

Michelle replied, "Let's do it."

So they did. Well, it wasn't that simple: Before starting the company, they worked on the concept with South Carolina's business school, did their market research, and raised money, experimenting until they had created sheets with better breathability, temperature control, moisture-wicking, and stretch than traditional ones.

BE SPECIFIC

It's important to know your audience. At its center, your story is about a specific idea or product or expertise that you're offering. You can't be all things to all people and still maintain your credibility and integrity. Make sure your story is crafted to appeal to the people you really want to become your supporters and that it draws from your core strength.

They called their product, and their company, SHEEX.

By August 2007, Susan and Michelle were ready to start selling. To do that, they used their story. After all, many people were selling sheets, but how many of them were former athletes and coaches selling ones that not only felt great but improved athletic performance by enhancing sleep?

The two women let their story pave their way. "We aren't people who just talk about athletics—we've *been* athletes. The retailers love it," Susan says. "It's also been the way we've made relationships with advisers. It opens doors—because of our sports background, we can find people we might not have been able to get to. And people ask Michelle all the time what it's like to play for Pat Summitt or ask me what Lou Holtz, Steve Spurrier, or Ray Tanner are like to work with."

SHEEX is off to a quick start: In June of 2009, the two women started selling online and in a few select retail stores in Houston. In 2010, they began national distribution through Brookstone catalogs and stores such as Bed Bath & Beyond and Sports Authority. In 2011, they'll hit the Home Shopping Network. "It's unusual to sell bedding through sporting-goods channels, but we've done extremely well, as this is where the customers, already sold on performance-fabric technology, are now sold on our story," says Michelle.

three

face your fears

Twenty years from now you will be more
disappointed by the things that you didn't do than
by the ones you did do. So throw off the bowlines. Sail
away from the safe harbor. Catch the trade winds in
your sails. Explore. Dream. Discover.

—MARK TWAIN

Here's a story about a woman I know who lived the typical life of a Texas suburbanite before she was inspired to help others, but who found that, to do so, she had to face her fears.

Pam met her husband, Mike, when she was just fourteen years old. They married several years later when Mike was a senior at Southern Methodist University; Pam then dropped out of college and helped support Mike through medical school by becoming a waitress. She soon gave birth to three kids, two boys and a girl, and became a stay-at-home mom.

Although Pam had considered a career in fashion, having kids sparked her interest in health, theirs and hers. She started to learn more about diet and exercise and became an avid aerobics fan, even competing in events. Her own health seemed excellent—until 1990, that is, when Pam went to the doctor and received the results of her lipid tests. Her cholesterol was a very high 242.

Pam exercised often and didn't smoke or drink, but she did eat a good deal of cheese, ice cream, and other foods containing saturated fats. She decided to cut most of them out of her diet. Within six months, her cholesterol had dropped to 146.

To help celebrate her achievement, Mike gave her a gift: a visit to *Shape* magazine's fitness camp in California, where regular people go to learn about fitness and health from professionals. Pam was thrilled but also terrified: She had never flown on an airplane by herself; she had never traveled *anywhere* by herself. But she wanted this vacation so badly that she managed to scare up the courage to fly, and she had a wonderful time, inspiring other women she met with the story of how she had lowered her cholesterol.

When Pam returned home, she felt motivated to do more. She didn't just want to tell her story to a few people; she wanted as many others as possible to learn from her experience. After batting around a few ideas, she decided to write a cookbook. Two days later, she dreamed up a logo: a bar of butter with a *Ghostbusters*-type symbol across it. *Butter Busters!*

That was the name of her book. Pam spent the following year writing it. When she was done, she faced another fear—what to do next. "I was so scared," she recalls. "I knew nothing about the publishing business. I had no idea at all what to do."

Without any connections to the New York publishing world, she decided the simplest, most direct way to solve her problem would be to publish the book herself. She scoured the yellow pages, visited a few printers, and found one whose owners seemed to be in such poor physical health that she felt sorry for them. Pam gave them the job because she thought that she could help them become healthier along the way—they, of all people, needed her book!

The owners quoted Pam $30,000 in printing costs. Because Pam and Mike didn't have that much extra money, Pam now faced another fear: going to the bank and taking out what seemed like an enormous loan.

She and Mike did it, however, and Pam was on her way. Sort of. This was in August of 1991. Pam wanted the book out by Christmas, but things were going poorly with the printer—very poorly. In fact, Pam started to show up every day to try to encourage the printers to finish the project, but it became clear that the company she had picked wasn't competent.

Finally, one rainy winter's day, Pam arrived at the printers' office and found the front doors locked tight, even though she could see the owners hiding inside. She called her husband, who had a friend on the police force, and they soon broke the door down, all to no avail. Even after a court battle, all Pam got back was her manuscript—the company had no money left for a refund.

Pam fell into a dark depression. This book was her mission—now what? Crying and sobbing, she lingered in her bedroom until finally Mike said, "This is enough. Let's go get another loan."

So the couple returned to the bank. Pam's project had now placed the family $60,000 in debt. Worse, Pam had to go find another printer. The last time she did that, she'd made a horribly costly misjudgment.

But Pam's new printer did a terrific job, and three weeks later Pam had 5,000 copies of the book ready to sell. The *Fort Worth Star-Telegram* published an article on her that was then syndicated around the country; a local television station interviewed her; and the 5,000 copies were sold out in three weeks. With her dining-room table as her office and her children doing the stamping, addressing, stuffing, and mailing, she then sold more and more books: 20,000 . . . 40,000 . . . 100,000. . . .

In just sixteen months, Pam had sold 450,000 copies of her *Butter Busters* cookbook. A large publishing company offered to fly her to New York, where they convinced her that the best way to reach an even wider audience—and therefore influence even more people to eat healthy—was to let them publish the book. She agreed.

The publisher sent Pam out on a book tour. Considering that the introverted Pam had to brace herself to talk to her small aerobics classes, this was a terrifying challenge. In fact, just before she was supposed to go on a four-week jaunt, she became so scared that she spent days hyperventilating and crying. If it weren't for the support of her family and her faith, she says, she couldn't have done it. But she went and summoned the courage to present her book, and her story, to the public. It worked. Eventually, *Butter Busters* sold 1.4 million copies.

Despite all her fears, Pam was able to see her original idea—writing a book to inspire others to eat healthy—not only come to fruition but also become a financial and inspirational success. "I knew what I was doing could change the lives of many people, and the desire to make that difference was stronger than all the fears that I kept having to face," she says.

The reason I know this story so well? Pam's last name is Mycoskie—she's my mom.

SABER-TOOTHED TIGERS AND BUSINESS PLANS

Fear is much more common than most people realize. That's because we live in a society where fear isn't something we like to talk about; as a rule, we're much more impressed by boldness. But fear happens, and it happens to everyone—especially anyone who is starting a business, interviewing for a job, or rallying people around a cause.

Fear stays with us throughout our lives. When we're unemployed, we fear that we'll never get another job. When we do get a job, we fear being fired. When we invest our earnings, we fear losing our savings. And when we start our own company, throwing in our own savings and efforts and faith, we fear losing everything.

Since fear is going to be with us for the rest of our lives, we must learn to face it, and the first step is understanding what fear is.

Fear happens when we feel anxious or apprehensive about a possible situation or event—in other words, something that hasn't even happened yet. It's our brain's way of telling us to pay attention and to alert us to dangers or risks. Without fear, our ancestors would have walked right up to a saber-toothed tiger or woolly mammoth and become that night's dinner. We no longer face prehistoric predators, but we still need to listen to fear when it warns us not to jump

A family photo taken during the first Shoe Drop. From left to right: my dad, Mike; my younger sister, Paige; my mom, Pam; me; and my younger brother, Tyler.

out of an airplane without a parachute, pick a fight with someone twice our size, or walk into a busy street without looking.

Fear also gives us a hormonal jolt that allows us to deal with urgent situations—the so-called "fight-or-flight" response, designed to launch us into action. But instead of responding to fear with action, too many people *stop* acting when they feel fear. They feel overwhelmed. They retreat. They give up. And often they use it as an excuse not to start something that matters.

This can be a terrible mistake. The fear generated by walking into the path of a ferocious saber-toothed tiger is very different from the fear of taking an intelligent business risk, but the tricky thing is that it might feel the same physiologically, and our reaction—to find some safe haven that spares us the horrible feeling of fear—might be the same. But we have to remember that the unsettling initial feeling of fear is not something we can control; it's completely natural. *Everyone* feels fear in business at some point, but the important thing to remember is that what you fear won't kill you, in business at least. Those who are successful face up to their fears and create a plan to overcome them.

In fact, the more you read about successful enterprises, the more you'll discover how many successful people, faced with rejection, bankruptcy, loss of support, or outright failure had every opportunity to shut down what they were doing and simply fold. Instead, they faced their fears, managed to get past them, and ultimately triumphed.

One of my favorite stories is that of Sam Walton, one of the most successful businessmen in all of history. In 1945 he owned what the *Harvard Business Review* would later call "a second-rate store in a second-rate town in what no one would have classified as a first-rate state." Many other such stores had failed, and this one seemed destined to join them. After all, Walton not only had little experience running a business, he'd also bought a store in a bad location, paid far too much for it, and signed a faulty lease.

In fact, he had far more than three strikes against him, and within a few years he was faced with total disaster. Yet despite all of his worst fears coming true, he managed to turn everything around and succeeded beyond anyone's wildest dreams. Today his store, Walmart, is one of the biggest companies in the world, and Walton became one of the world's wealthiest men. Why? According to the *Harvard Business Review* article, "The real explanation for his success was that he had the courage of his convictions." His belief in his discount business model—in spite of his opening blunders—carried him past what could have been a permanent barrier of fear.

Everyone who succeeds battles through adversity. The more you read biographies, talk to successful people, and listen to business leaders speak, the more you'll hear about mistakes, screwups, fears, and failures. But you'll also see that those downers often turn out to be the biggest blessings they ever received. This is a lesson you have to keep learning.

I guarantee that in any new endeavor, there will be days you'll feel completely doomed, convinced that failure is inevitable and that, no matter how hard you work, you will never succeed. I had plenty of these days during the first few years of TOMS. We were doing something totally different and it was scary. When that does happen, you will be faced with one of the most important tests you'll ever encounter. Setbacks and fear are inevitable. The thing that distinguishes the ultimate successes from the ultimate failures is this: What do you do with them?

This is the moment when too many people turn back, give up, or start thinking of excuses for or explanations of why they should call it quits. I completely understand this instinct.

Fear is one of our most powerful emotions, and the more we focus on it, the more it grows and distorts our behavior. But there's a way through it. Instead of focusing on the fear itself, which you cannot control, focus on what you *can* control: your actions. How you react to negative feelings will be the key to your success. Becoming comfortable with fear, and acting confidently in its face, will not only give you more courage when facing it next time but also greatly increase your chances of achieving success and happiness. Here's how another first-time entrepreneur dealt with it.

THE VEEV FEAR FACTOR

Courtney Reum didn't start off in business thinking about rain forests. The thirty-two-year-old Columbia University grad, who'd double-majored in economics and philosophy, went straight to Wall Street, becoming an investment banker at Goldman Sachs with a subspecialty in consumer products.

But a few years later, after working with start-up brands including Under Armour and Vitaminwater, Courtney decided to leave Goldman to become an entrepreneur. Having worked peripherally on the ten-plus-billion-dollar merger of liquor companies Pernod Ricard and Allied Domecq, the former banker became interested in the spirits market, where there seemed to be a lack of innovation.

And so, in late 2007, Courtney and brother Carter started VeeV, a spirit with the tagline "A better way to drink." The reason it's better, says Courtney, is that it is infused with açaí berries, which are loaded with vitamins C and E. Furthermore, for every bottle sold, VeeV donates one dollar to rain forest preservation through the Sustainable Açaí Project, founded by fellow açaí entrepreneurs at Sambazon (Sustainable Management of the Brazilian Amazon). VeeV also operates the only distillery to get its energy through renewable wind power. Finally, VeeV is the first spirits company ever to offset the carbon-dioxide emissions of its business activities and become certified carbon neutral.

The company's sales have been excellent, increasing more than 250 percent year over year, and VeeV is on its way to becoming one of the bestselling new brands in the country.

Like nearly everyone who starts a company, Courtney was sometimes scared: "I would wake up from those three-in-the-morning nightmares. It became apparent pretty quickly that we didn't know much about the spirits business, and we had much to learn. We also didn't know if anyone else might have a copycat product in the works; we were, in a word, terrified."

Here are some tips Courtney has shared with me over the years to help face and then fight off fear:

NO MATTER WHAT HAPPENS, WIN, LOSE, OR DRAW, NEVER FORGET THAT LIFE GOES ON

Courtney explains: "It was scary leaving Goldman, but as frightening as that was, the fact was, when we started VeeV, I was twenty-seven years old. I thought, *What if all this is a terrible failure—what would be the worst that could happen?* I would wake up at thirty having had an amazing experience and be ready to do something else. In other words, the downside is not as bad as people think. While a financial failure can be disheartening and difficult to deal with, your career path may yet be brighter: I know many entrepreneurs who have failed, but they also succeeded because, based on their experiences of starting and running a company, they are now being offered much more interesting jobs than people who never took those risks."

DON'T FEAR THE UNKNOWN

"People fear the unknown, but the truth is, everything is unknown by definition—no one really knows what they are getting themselves into. When we started VeeV, we had no idea what would happen. Neither my brother nor I knew anything about the alcohol industry; we didn't even know what a distributor was, much less where to find one.

"People tend to think that they should start something only when they are totally and completely knowledgeable about the field they want to enter. That probably will never happen. No one goes into these ventures knowing everything. You have a good idea, you have energy, you raise money, and you do your best. If you spend all your time learning and studying to be ready, you'll never stop learning and studying. And you'll never start your venture."

EVERYONE MAKES MISTAKES

"When people start something new, they often become so scared of making mistakes, they come down with Analysis Paralysis. They become so fixated on the idea that every decision matters so much that they obsess over each one and ultimately do nothing. Rather than let the boat stall, I'd always keep it moving in some direction. A few mistakes will seldom sink the entire ship. You may get a hole in the boat and start taking on water, but you aren't going to drown. In general, there is virtually no mistake you can make early on that you can't recover from."

DON'T WORRY ABOUT WHAT OTHERS THINK

"I'm sure some people at Goldman, when they found out about VeeV, sneered and said, 'Courtney just can't hack it.' So what? My brother and I may not be making as much money as these people (if they're still in the business). But we're doing something we really care about and that we love. That's worth it. Yes, it was rough at first, thinking about what people would say. Then it occurred to me: I am never going to see these people again."

DON'T FALL VICTIM TO THE BEST IDEA FREEZE

"Many people starting something new are intimidated by the question 'Is this the best idea I have?' Of course a good idea is a great start, but the success of most ventures actually lies in the execution phase, not in the idea. I'd take a decent idea and superb execution over a great idea with sub-par execution any day of the week."

THE FEAR KILLERS

Now that TOMS is growing and is more financially secure, I don't feel the same kind of fear I felt in the beginning. But writing this book has brought back some of the scarier memories, such as when TOMS didn't have the money to pay our bills and we had to ask all of our vendors to extend us credit beyond what was normally accepted. I remember daily meetings with Justin, my numbers guy, trying to decide which vendor would be paid that week. (It usually ended up being the person who yelled the loudest when Justin was pleading with them for more time.) Our line of credit was almost always fully drawn, our credit cards were maxed out, and our bank was always asking about when we were going to pay off our debts. Then there was the pressure of having to sell and give away the shoes.

What was most frightening, though, was that, given all the press we'd received and our bold declaration that we were changing the concept of business and philanthropy, we were being watched closely. A failure would have been very public.

But I found some effective ways to live with the fear until I could overcome it. First, I remembered to live my story.

I went back to my core question: Why am I doing this?

When you go back to your core motivations, you affirm the authenticity of your project, which takes away one of the biggest fears: that you are a fraud. When you live your story, you don't have to pretend you're someone you're not. You can just be yourself. It's been said that there's nothing more dangerous than someone who has nothing to lose—and it's true in business too. When you are living your story, it means your actions and your mission are the same, which eliminates any room for shame or disappointment, the two emotions that underlie our greatest fears. That's when you have nothing to lose.

I also made sure to surround myself with interns. The wonderful thing about interns is that they are so enthusiastic and new to everything that they don't waste time being fearful. They're just excited to be working on something that feels important and meaningful. Having a group of enthusiastic people around you, all busy working toward the success of your enterprise, gives you confidence, makes you feel legitimate, and, ultimately, helps make whatever idea you are trying to create a reality. Thrive on interns, who can challenge your ideas and make you feel young and confident, no matter how old and scared you are.

I surround myself with inspirational quotations. This easy-to-follow piece of advice has played a huge role in my being able to get past my own fears and insecurities throughout my entrepreneurial career. Say you're starting a company, and you don't have the money to hire a high-powered assistant or a board of directors or anyone at all who could give you advice, motivate you, or just be a sounding board for your ideas. You still have the ability to seek out amazing help.

Original intern Jonathan and me learning how to make shoes at our first factory in Argentina.

How? Quotes. Quotes from people who have seen their way through fear and failure and still risen. Surround yourself with these powerful words.

When I started in business, I was often lonely, so I placed favorite quotes all over my apartment. They made me feel like I was never really alone. I would type up and print out my favorites on a piece of paper or cut them out of magazines and tape them to my wall. For the first six years of my entrepreneurial life, these quotes were all over my apartment, making it look as if a paper tornado had flown past.

Here are a few of my favorite quotes about fear that have helped me through some of my darkest times:

Change your thoughts and you change your world.
—Norman Vincent Peale

Many of life's failures are people who did not realize how close they were to success when they gave up.
—Thomas Edison

Success is the ability to go from one failure to another with no loss of enthusiasm.
—Winston Churchill

You gain strength, courage and confidence by every experience in which you really stop to look fear in the face. You are able to say to yourself, 'I lived through this horror. I can take the next thing that comes along.' . . . You must do the thing you think you cannot do.
—Eleanor Roosevelt

In addition to surrounding myself with short quotes, I read biographies. Because I left college to start a business and never received my degree, much of my education came from books that I found on my own, not the ones assigned to me by professors. My favorite books have always been biographies of successful entrepreneurs and other inspiring people.

For example, when I started my cable-television business, I made a point to read the biography and autobiography of every figure in the business I could find, like that of Ted Turner, who founded CNN. When I started TOMS, I read about Richard Branson (founder of Virgin), Yvon Chouinard (founder of Patagonia), Mary Kay (founder of Mary Kay Cosmetics), Herb Kelleher (CEO of Southwest Airlines), Howard Schultz (CEO of Starbucks), and others whose businesses were devoted to both profit and a larger mission.

When I advise you to read biographies, I don't mean only in book form. There is plenty of biographical material on the Internet. Say you're thinking about starting a nonprofit focused on protecting the environment or are about to change jobs at a late stage in your career. You'll probably be able to find stories by or about people who have done (or who are doing) something similar to what you have in mind. Learning how someone else is already doing the thing you want to do, or a version of it, can eliminate fear—every path is easier to follow when you see someone else's footprints already on it.

I also remember to think small. It's best not to regard your next step as a tremendous risk. Think about it as one small step on a long journey.

Thinking big always sounds good, but it's a common mistake shared by lots of people starting a business. We started TOMS with 250 pairs of shoes in three duffel bags—that's it. I didn't quit my job immediately. I didn't invest tens of thousands of dollars. I just made 250 pairs of shoes and tried to sell them.

By starting small, you can work through your story, try out your idea, and test your mettle. There's a Japanese concept known as *kaizen*, which says that small improvements made every day will lead to massive improvement overall. This idea was made famous in the 1980s by Japanese car manufacturers, who very slowly but surely established a dominant position in the American automobile market by adding small improvements to their vehicles rather than introducing revolutionary innovation. When you keep this concept in mind, reaching big goals seems much less scary.

Starting small is a particularly good idea for someone who already has a job. Let's say you're a math teacher but your real passion is baking. You don't have to resign your position. Instead, rather than sitting on the beach for your next vacation, volunteer for a week at a bakery to see if you enjoy it. Learn what you can without making a full commitment. Ask the owner if you can take on part-time evening or weekend work in which you can learn the trade while still making money at your day job.

If you discover that you are skilled at and passionate about your side project, you can then take the next step knowing much more than if you started blind, even as you still have much to learn.

I would also write down my fears and look at them.

When fears stay stuck inside your head, your imagination can go wild, torturing you with all the various negative possibilities and outcomes. But when you write them down, you clarify exactly what you are afraid of, and soon the power they hold over you will fade.

Whenever I feel fear coming on, I create a what-if scenario by drawing a line down the middle of a piece of yellow legal paper, using the left side to list my fears and the right to imagine the worst possible outcome.

For example, when I began TOMS, I wrote on one side: "If no one buys the shoes, then the following will happen: I will lose $5,000 in material and start-up costs. Three months of my life will result in little."

On the other side, I wrote:

"Even if worse comes to worst, I'll be in Argentina for three months, learn a new skill, make new friends, and have great fun."

My final fear killer is to seek as much advice as I can—from everyone. You can often get great advice from all kinds of people if you just ask. Yes, some people probably won't talk to you, no matter how intelligently you approach them. But you'd be surprised how many are more than happy to help.

Using the Internet, you can reach almost anyone. And because the Web offers a low-commitment way to communicate, successful people are more likely than before to give advice. In the past, you had to cold-call, set up a meeting, arrange for transportation, deal with logistics, and so on. Now you can write an email and in minutes receive great advice.

I've found that people like to give advice to those with

whom they empathize or in whom they see a version of themselves. So many times I've seen young women reach out to successful female entrepreneurs and get terrific advice because the latter identify with a version of themselves in

PRO'S	CON'S
① A new challenge	① Not sure if people will like shoe
② Could help a lot of kids	
③ get to spend more time in Argentina	② would have to say NO to Carl on new venture
④ shoes are really comfortable, so if does not work, could give as christmas gifts to friends	③ No guarantee model can work
	④ Not sure we can grow production if it does
⑤ easy to test by selling online b in a few stores in LA	⑤ $ $?
⑥ Always wanted to be more involved in charity	
⑦ I have never been so excited about ANYTHING!	

former times. Remember, once you become successful, life can become a little dry—the adventure and danger are reduced. So when a younger version of an entrepreneur comes along, his or her mentor gets to live vicariously through that person's start-up phase—and play a role in the success of a new project.

In 2002, after competing on *The Amazing Race* and experiencing firsthand the phenomenon of reality television's amazing popularity, I decided to create a 24/7 reality-television cable channel. After doing a great deal of research, I contacted a man named Jack Crosby, a pioneer in the cable TV business. Like me, Jack was from Texas, and like me, he'd been in his mid-twenties when he started his first cable venture—and today he is in the cable television hall of fame. He soon became my mentor. Not only did he give me excellent advice, but he got a kick out of living vicariously through my battles, fondly remembering what he had gone through forty years earlier.

THE TIMING IS NEVER RIGHT

One of the key fears that we all have is fear that this is the wrong time to start whatever our project is and we should wait until the "time is right." Tim Ferriss, author of the bestselling *The 4-Hour Workweek*, has this to say about timing: "For all the most important things, the timing always sucks. Waiting for a good time to quit your job? The stars will never align and the traffic lights of life will never all be green at the same time. The universe doesn't conspire against you, but it doesn't go out of its way to line up all the pins either. Conditions are never perfect. 'Someday' is a disease that will take your dreams to the grave with you. . . . If it's important to you and you want to do it 'eventually,' just do it and correct course along the way."

If you wait for the timing to be right before you make a move, you may never make a move at all. As a rule, you can pretty much count on time to create some of the scariest moments in your business career. It certainly happened to me.

Another of my early mentors was an entrepreneur named Carl Westcott. Carl has started many companies, from 1-800-FLOWERS to Westcott Communications, which he sold for a ton of money; he was also an early investor in satellite radio and various online businesses.

I originally met Carl by cold-calling him and his son, Court, when I was trying to raise money for the reality-TV cable channel. Carl agreed to talk because Court was interested in cable TV, and he himself had made a great deal of money with closed-circuit cable programming. It turned out he didn't want to invest in my company (he saw too many risks—and he was right), but he liked me enough to start a business relationship anyway.

The company he was working on at the time was called Digital Witness; it was a very successful start-up that helped restaurant managers monitor their employees. In 2006, Carl asked me to run his West Coast operation. This was a huge opportunity: It came with a large salary plus a small percentage of the company, and, even better, Carl was the person for whom I most wanted to work.

Unfortunately, this offer arrived just before my trip to

Argentina. The next time I saw Carl, back in America, he asked for my decision. I was terrified. I didn't want to lose my relationship with him. And I didn't want to lose the guaranteed financial security of a high-paying job in exchange for a risky start-up.

But I felt so passionate about TOMS and knew I would never feel good about myself if I didn't give it a shot. So I turned down Carl's offer. But I did give his family the first pairs of TOMS prototype shoes ever made. Carl and Court, the serial entrepreneurs, are still holding on to them. When I asked them why, they said, "Simple—if you continue the way you've been going, one day these shoes could be worth a fortune on eBay."

be resourceful without resources

Imagination is more important than knowledge.

—ALBERT EINSTEIN

When TOMS started, we had what could only be called very limited resources. Actually, it might be more accurate to say we had just about none.

Because the concept of giving a product away to match a product sold was unique, we had no proven model to convince others to back us. The truth is, we didn't even know if it would work; therefore, it was difficult for us to raise money the way someone starting a traditional business does. Instead, we kept explaining the idea over and over again to number-crunching wizards trained to make investment decisions based on the potential for profit, not philosophy.

With no money, no likelihood of raising it, and no proven business model, we had to cut more corners than corners existed.

As mentioned, one of the first things I did—and this was when TOMS' entire workforce in America consisted of me—was to place an ad for interns on craigslist. The ad offered summer internships in design and marketing and referred people to the TOMS website, which was quite nice—nice enough to make it seem as if we were the real deal.

> POSTING ID: 143649614
>
> REPLY TO: tomsshoes@gmail.com
>
> SUBJECT: (marketing jobs) Hip Shoe Company seeks SUPER FANTASTIC Interns!
>
> If you are smart, creative, and entrepreneurial minded, this is a fantastic opportunity . . .
>
> TOMS is an up-and-coming shoe company based in Venice, California. Our product line is a fusion of Argentine fashion and California Surf Culture. For every shoe that we sell, we will give a FREE pair to a less fortunate person in Latin America or Africa.
>
> Our company is looking to fill several positions:
>
> 1. SUPER FANTASTIC Business Intern—The person chosen for this position will work directly with the CEO

of TOMS. No coffee making. You will have a huge hand in advertising, marketing, brand development, and distribution.

2. WEB DESIGN Intern—Must be an experienced and AMAZING Design Student. Your work will directly affect the growth of our business. This is a great opportunity to build your resume.

Although this is a non-paid internship, there is a very serious chance that this could lead to a lucrative full time job.

For more information, please send resume to tomsshoes @gmail.com.

Thanks!
Blake Mycoskie

Many people applied, excited at the prospect of learning so much at what must have sounded like a strange and interesting company. But when they showed up at the company headquarters—aka my apartment—for many, the excitement quickly evaporated.

At the time, my Venice neighborhood was more welcoming to drug dealers than to young summer interns. In fact, to let applicants into the apartment, I had to usher them past a somber-looking, barbed wire fence. Then I sat them down at the kitchen table where they might see the remains of that morning's breakfast tacos next to a few pairs of shoes and a bunch of papers. Those who had pictured a more traditional internship—a big company filled with hip young professionals—didn't pan out. But a few applicants recognized that this was a chance to get in on the ground floor of something that could really take off.

TOMS' first three interns started in May, and then we took on three more in July. One of them was my brother, Tyler—families are excellent places to raid for resources.

Because we weren't paying anyone yet, we made up for the lack of funds in fun. We would work hard and then play hard. Sometimes the two collided: Once, after a very late night at the apartment, Tyler fell asleep in my bedroom and slept in the next day. Meanwhile, I had to get up early for an appointment, and Jonathan was meeting with our UPS regional rep (UPS was one of our few vendors at the time). Because my apartment was our office, we held meetings in my bedroom, where we had placed two desks (the kitchen and living room were filled with boxes and shoes to be shipped out).

About ten minutes after they started the meeting, a white-sheeted, ghostlike creature arose from my bed. The woman from UPS screamed.

It was Tyler, waking up—they hadn't noticed that he was asleep beside them under a heap of bedding. Luckily, he was wearing clothes. And the UPS rep turned out to be a good sport, once she calmed down.

The apartment had two other bedrooms, occupied by my two roommates. Both of these guys had nine-to-five jobs, so when they went to work, I turned our home into the TOMS office. The roomies were cool with this as long as everyone was gone and the apartment was clean when they came home by six o'clock. And they didn't want us to use their bedrooms, which was fair.

Because the place was small and we had boxes all over, that summer I decided to move my office outside into the yard, where I placed a desk and a chair. As a result of being outside all day, I looked tanner than I ever had before. When people came to meet Jonathan, they would walk past me and then ask him, "Who's the random dude out there in surf trunks?"

However, as business picked up, we had to use the room-mates' bedrooms; there was no other space left. The guys knew it, but because at the end of each day we ran around making the rooms look absolutely immaculate, they didn't say anything.

Well, almost immaculate. The person whose room we used the most was Jimmy, then the president of my online driver-ed company. After running that company all day, Jimmy would come home wanting to chill, only to find little cardboard shavings littered throughout his room. That was the one thing we couldn't always clean up—those tiny pieces of padding that fall out of boxes. Because Jimmy was anal about cleanliness, the little pieces drove him crazy. For nine months he was frustrated, but because he paid the least in rent, he did his best to cope. (It's a good thing his frustration didn't get the best of him, because we ended up hiring him to run our international sales.)

When we got our first big media hits and stores started calling with orders, TOMS had only three interns and me and our low-rent infrastructure. We owned one cordless phone with a constantly dying battery, so no one could talk long when prospective customers called. Whenever the phone rang, whoever was closest would answer.

One day it rang, and since I was nearest, I said, "Hello, TOMS Shoes."

The man on the other end of the phone was very nervous. "I'm calling from Nordstrom," he said. "I need to place a test order for one hundred pairs immediately."

Now, Nordstrom is known for having an incredible shoe department. It can take years for the company to even hold a meeting with you. But the man on the phone said that his boss had seen TOMS featured in a fashion magazine, and that shoppers were already coming into stores asking for them as a result. So he wanted to try us out.

"I'm an assistant buyer," the man continued. "My boss is on my back. I need to get this order processed right away."

"I would love to send them to you," I said, "but we don't have any shoes now." This was true.

"No, you don't understand," he said. "This is Nordstrom calling. I need the shoes immediately."

"Sir," I said, "I don't have any."

The man started to get a little testy. "Just put me in touch with the sales department," he snapped. "Right now."

Not sure what to do, I tossed the phone to one of the interns. She shrugged. "Hi," she said. "This is the sales department."

The Nordstrom guy repeated the same rap for the intern—he didn't know we were all sitting in one small room—and she in turn repeated what I had said. The man became so frustrated that this time he demanded to speak to customer service. So the intern handed the phone over to another intern.

But before the Nordstrom buyer could complain again, the next intern said, "Look, that first guy you talked to was the company founder, the second person was an intern, and I'm just another intern."

The guy finally laughed. "You guys are that small?"

"Yes, we are," he said.

The man couldn't do anything but wait, and in two weeks we sent him the shoes. Today, Nordstrom is one of our largest customers.

THE ENCHANTED GARAGE

These stories are not just fun to tell, they also capture the excitement and sense of possibility that compensate for the deprivations and anxiety of the start-up period. Many of the greatest business stories in recent history have similar creation myths—usually involving a magical space called "the garage" (and for "garage" you can substitute "apartment," "basement," "attic," or even "car"). Starting up in a small, improvised space is not only fun but can be an advantage with interns and early employees. For one thing, by operating out of an unconventional space, you're automatically lowering their expectations. No one expects an immediate financial reward from an internship or start-up gig, particularly one that shares its office space with the family car; everyone is excited to be a part of something new. And, unlike working out of an office, working out of the garage makes everyone feel equal; there are no corner offices or other perks to compete for, so the pecking-order mentality disappears. Everyone feels they are part of one team, and that helps create a great company culture from the start.

Many of the greatest companies in the world were started out of a metaphorical garage. Bert and John Jacobs, founders of the apparel brand Life is good, got their start selling shirts out of the back of their van. Kenneth Cole's first shoe display was in the trunk of his car. Two guys named Ben and Jerry, with $8,000 in savings and a $4,000 loan, leased an old gas station in Burlington, Vermont, as their first ice-cream store. Mark Zuckerberg co-created Facebook in his Harvard dorm room. Kevin Rose began Digg in his apartment. Reid Hoffman began LinkedIn in his living room. And Steve Jobs initiated Apple in his actual family garage.

But this isn't just a recent phenomenon. In fact, almost all of the successful brands that people love and adore began with few resources. For example, in 1950s California, Ruth and Elliot Handler started a picture-frame business in their garage. They also made dollhouse furniture with excess material and soon realized that toys were more profitable than picture frames. After 1955, they released a doll to go with that toy furniture—her name was Barbie. Their company: Mattel.

Also in the 1950s, there was a man in Detroit who lived on the top floor of his home with his family while using the bottom floor as a recording studio; he eventually expanded to his garage. Soon artists such as Diana Ross and the Supremes, the Temptations, Stevie Wonder, and Gladys Knight and the Pips were dropping by—the garage belonged to Berry Gordy, Jr., the founder of Motown Records; it is now part of the Motown Historical Museum.

IMAGINATION TRUMPS MONEY

A lack of resources is no reason to avoid starting a company. If anything, it often inspires creativity and a competitive edge. Even though they may have excellent ideas, many people still believe that they can't start a business because they don't have enough of everything else. But our lack of resources when we started TOMS is one of the reasons we've succeeded. How can that be?

Being comfortable can hurt your creative entrepreneurial spirit. An early and unearned sense of security can be the worst thing that can happen to a business. If you have little money and have to bootstrap and improvise to pull things together, that becomes embedded in your company's DNA forever—so as you scale up, you maintain the frugality and efficiency that helped you survive your earliest days. For instance, now that TOMS is an established, successful business, we could throw resources around with a little less care than we used to, but we don't. We still emphasize creative problem-solving and are scrupulous with our expenditures. Our culture is lean and mean—well, maybe not mean. But being creative and resourceful are skills we honed in our hungry days, and they are just as useful now. It's an impulse that can lead to extraordinary success.

For instance, in 2001, a man named Tom Szaky was looking for a bottle in which to put the product he was selling—liquefied worm-poop fertilizer—and decided that even the cheapest bottling options were too expensive. He found that discarded plastic soda bottles, which were essentially free, worked fine. He soon started TerraCycle, a company that produces a natural plant food made from worm waste packaged in reused containers, many of which are collected through fund-raising programs. Today the company also repurposes waste packaging into new products ranging from cellphone holders to messenger bags, thereby reducing the amount of waste that goes into our nation's landfills. In the decade since the company started, its sales have more than doubled each year and its products can now be found in

Bootstrapping our first trade show with a homemade booth at the Action Sports Retailers show (ASR) in San Diego.

Home Depot, Target, Walgreens, OfficeMax, and Walmart, among many other locations.

Szaky funded the early days of his start-up by winning business-plan competitions and he saved money by hiring a team of thirty-five dedicated interns and housing them all in one house, where they slept three or four to a room. Szaky would personally wake up each intern in the morning, blasting Vanilla Ice music over the loudspeakers.

According to renowned Silicon Valley venture capitalist Mike Maples, companies that start off overfunded actually are in more danger of faltering than those that are underfunded; too much money, he says, is not only unnecessary, but also toxic. Maples points out the inverse relationship between the amount of money an entrepreneur spends at start-up and the business's ultimate success. It's no coincidence that blue-chip companies like Cisco, Google, Facebook, Digg, and even Microsoft began as hyperfrugal start-ups.

Yes, it's hard to turn down money. But if you raise more than you really need, you'll probably end up with a three-bin copy machine when one bin would do, or a fancy telephone system when cellphones would do just as well. Or you might create fancy positions, hire extraneous personnel, like vice presidents who don't do anything except hand out business cards that say they're a vice president. Worst of all, that money comes with strings attached: You'll have to answer to investors who tell you how to run your business but might not share your core values.

Some of the most interesting business failures in the last decade were companies that simply had too much cash. Who knows what might have happened to Pets.com, for instance, if it had had limited resources? Instead, the firm, formed in 1998 as a pioneering Internet pet-supply store, managed to capture more than $300 million in venture capital—so much money that it was able to buy a multimillion-dollar television ad aired during the Super Bowl in January 2000. But no matter how much money the company made—which wasn't much—Pets.com just kept burning through their capital. According to *Thinking Inside the Box*, by Kirk Cheyfitz, the online company spent $11.8 million in advertising in its first fiscal year while generating only $619,000 in rev-

SEAN'S FRUGALITY

Falling Whistles is a nonprofit organization that campaigns for peace in the Democratic Republic of the Congo. It was started in 2009 by a young man named Sean Carasso, who was inspired by his experiences when he went on TOMS' second Shoe Drop—and who has since become a friend of mine.

Afterward Sean decided he wanted to make a difference, and while traveling in Africa, he came up with an idea: Falling Whistles, which sells whistles for $34 to $104 to raise money for education, advocacy, and the rehabilitation of war-affected people. (The name comes from Sean's conversation with a former child soldier who told him of children sent into battle armed with whistles.) In 2010, Falling Whistles opened an office in Washington, D.C.; a year later it was helping advocate for free elections in Congo, and it continues to do everything it can to help people understand Congolese politics.

Sean started Falling Whistles with five dollars. With that money he and some friends bought "five crappy whistles from the surplus store. We sold those, and we had $50. We went and bought more crappy whistles and we had $150." With that money they eventually were able to organize a fund-raiser and begin to build a coalition of supporters.

enue. By the fall of 2000, Pets.com had collapsed. What if it had started more simply and grown organically? Their idea wasn't terrible—today there are viable online pet-supply operations—but clearly their execution had some flaws. Perhaps if they hadn't had so much capital, they could have been more entrepreneurial and successful.

Similarly, Webvan.com started with a solid idea—home grocery delivery—that allowed it to raise a great deal of money even though the grocery industry historically has very thin margins. Webvan started in 1999 in Foster City, California, and immediately expanded to eight additional

Sean says that his father taught him the most important lesson in business: "If you spend less than you make, you will always be profitable." Sean and his team did everything they could to spend less. "I had a friend in Houston who read my journal entry on his iPhone. We had a conversation the next day. He sold his company the next week, packed up his car, and drove to L.A. to run finance for us for free."

And: "We put out the word that we needed interns; we had eight kids show up in our front yard and say, 'We'll do whatever it takes.'"

And: "We lived on nothing. We ate Top Ramen and spaghetti for a year and slept in bunk beds. We started in a house where we were stuffing six people into three bedrooms. We had our office in the garage."

In that last office, Sean threw a housewarming/office launch party and asked people to bring any extra supplies they had. "We got a whiteboard and whiteboard markers. Printer paper, an old printer. Coffee mugs, coffeemaker . . . the basics.

"Not having any resources in the beginning has made us much better at everything we do. It's made us more frugal with our money, more responsible with our time and staff, more focused with our partnerships in Congo and the States. Learning to survive is one of the best lessons in entrepreneurialism. You just have to make magic every day."

cities by 2001, with plans in place to enter twenty-six more. It had been able to raise $320 million in capital by going public, but between its expensive warehouse infrastructure, 2,000 paid employees, and other high expenses, the company folded later in 2001. Years later, companies like Fresh-Direct have succeeded in the exact same market by building their businesses slowly and intelligently.

eToys was another unfortunate story of the dot-com bubble—one more company founded in the late 1990s that raised a lot of money and had tons of press. Its stock rocketed from twenty to seventy-six dollars on its first day of trading, but, like Pets.com, eToys spent millions on advertising and marketing, far more than it made in sales, and the owners filed for Chapter 11 bankruptcy protection in 2001 (although the name is back in business under new ownership). Meanwhile, Amazon.com, Toys "Я" Us, and Walmart have all successfully entered the online toy business over the years and the market has grown dramatically.

THEY CALL IT GOOD KARMA FOR A REASON

At TOMS, we tried to make the best of our limited resources through one of the most nontraditional means ever: From day one, we wanted to help those in need. That odd beginning led to customer loyalty that in turn helped make our business thrive.

If you incorporate giving into your business model, and

give your business a mission larger than your bottom line, you also create opportunities that companies with more resources might not be able to enjoy. If it weren't for this model, AT&T, Theory, Ralph Lauren, and all our other partners would not have approached us to collaborate. People want to feel they are making a difference, and few things make them more likely to provide a discount or a break than knowing they're giving something back—not to a company but to the community at large.

Unfortunately, many people think they can't give anything away when they start a business because they have nothing to give. Nor, they fear, can they afford to share a percentage of profits, because they don't have any profits yet. But that's the very reason you *should* do it: Without resources, you will need a lot of other people's help, and the best way to get that help is to stand for something bigger than just yourself and your business.

Remember, in this era when so many of us spend our work and personal hours sitting alone with our computers and digital devices, people want to be part of something that throws them back into the world and connects them to other people—even if they won't make money on it. There are lots of ways to get people invested in your project. Think of the online user-editable encyclopedia Wikipedia. It started with very few resources—and even now is run quite frugally—but it gave people an opportunity to become part of its creation. Once people found out they could publish their expertise on Wikipedia, offering and exchanging ideas with the world, its resources pool jumped exponentially. It now has thousands of unpaid volunteers, who've become a part of something great and lasting.

MAKE WHAT YOU HAVE COUNT

Here are some other ways to amplify limited resources:

DEVELOP A PRESENCE WHERE IT'S FREE

Social media barely existed a decade ago; today these sites are a force that can't be ignored. Facebook, LinkedIn, foursquare, Gowalla, Twitter, and a host of new sites every day allow people to interact easily and freely.

The best thing about social media is that you don't need money to benefit from them fully. They are the great leveling factor between companies with resources and those without. Today, TOMS has a greater social-media presence on Facebook and Twitter than most Fortune 500 companies do. For many large companies, social media are a secondary form of brand maintenance, if not an afterthought. For us they are built into the very DNA of our business.

SPACE MATTERS

When I moved to Los Angeles, I was working in the entertainment business, brokering product-placement deals and starting my all-reality cable channel—and living on a

FREE SPEECH

In the beginning, everything at TOMS was free—or at least we wanted it to be. The goal was to get as much of what we needed as possible without spending any money. Often we did that by explaining our business model, letting people know that if they helped us we would be able to give away more shoes.

Since my parents live in Texas, my good friend and trusted adviser Liz Heller serves as my L.A. mom, helping TOMS in numerous ways. She is also the one who taught me so much about free help. TOMS borrowed her vocabulary as well, coining new terms for free stuff: a free lunch became a "frunch," as in "I got a great frunch today." "Frinsurance" is free insurance, "frinstillations" are free installations, "fregal" is free legal advice, and "frent" free rent. Still more—"fromotion": free promotion. "Frar": a free car rental. "Framples": free samples. And whether we got what we wanted or not, this mentality helped keep us frugal.

friend's couch. I didn't have much in the way of resources. But I knew that if people were going to take me seriously, a powerful Hollywood address and an office couldn't hurt.

In those days, I was spending a lot of time at a coffee shop called Cyberjava, on Hollywood Boulevard, where the waitstaff and I became friendly. I made a deal with them to let me print their address on my business card and start receiving my mail there. I also used their fax machine; one of the waitresses would even answer my phone occasionally, saying, "Mycoskie Media, how can I help you?" As far as the world was concerned, I had an office on Hollywood Boulevard.

Office space is the single biggest waste of money when businesses start out. As the examples of garage-based ventures show, most start-ups don't need physical administrative space or expensive long-term leases, which are both unnecessary given today's easy telecommunications and executive services. But when you need an address, there are creative ways of getting one.

FORGET TITLES

I have never believed in conventional titles. At one of my previous companies, my title was Believer. People would ask why, and I would reply that I really believed in the value of what we did. An interesting title can go a long way.

At TOMS, everyone has a title containing the word "shoe." I am Chief Shoe Giver. Candice Wolfswinkel, who in the early days helped hold our company together, is Shoe Glue. My super assistant, Megan, is Straight Shoeter.

Some of our other shoe-related titles: Shoe Chef. Shoe Lace. Cash Shoe. Shoe Dude. Shoe-per-Woman.

When you dispose of formal titles, no one knows the pecking order. Both an executive vice president and an intern can have solid-sounding titles. This framework forces people from outside the company to treat everyone they meet as though they were the most important person in the company—because they don't know they're not. Innovative titles offer a great way to gain access or tap resources from nothing: I can let a recently graduated twenty-two-year-old with the title of Shoe Provider talk to the senior buyer at a major department store. The latter sees only a funny title and for all they know, the person on the other end of the phone has twenty years of experience.

Also, if you are starting a new organization by yourself, calling yourself founder and/or CEO makes your company look small, clearly identifying you as the only person within the organization. At another of my earlier companies, one that I founded and led, my card read "Vice President of Sales." If you call yourself a vice president, it implies that there's also a CEO and/or president out there and you're just one part of a larger staff.

In the long run, titles are simply a way to get the job done. If a new employee can call herself the vice president of partnership and can use that title to get in the door with a big prospect, why not let her be vice president of partnership? Tomorrow she can be something else.

BUSINESS CARDS MEAN BUSINESS

When you're starting out, a business card may well be the only thing that leaves a lingering impression. Here's one area where it might benefit you to spend a little extra money. A truly interesting card can be impressive and help someone remember you who otherwise might not. Cards can be in strange shapes, funny sizes, and weird colors. I once saw someone whose business card was a metal coin imprinted with his information. I bet few people threw that one away. Another card I will always remember was made of biodegradable paper and a seed, so you could plant it and watch it grow.

But you can also take advantage of not having a business card at all. The most interesting thing I ever did with business cards was to recycle someone else's. While working on a new media venture, I had a meeting with a group of potential investors; afterward we all exchanged business cards. Instead of handing out my own cards, I took the cards

Dear Craig,

I want to thank you so much for setting up your website. If it were not for you, starting TOMS would have been much more difficult. Here is a list of all the ways we have used Craigslist. Please send me your shoe size, and I will gladly send you a pair of TOMS!

Carpe Diem,

BlaKE
Chief Shoe Giver
TOMS SHOES

1. Our 1st interns
2. many of our employees
3. most of our furniture
4. models for our photo shoots
5. local artists to design TOMS at Style your sole events
6. Seamstresses to make curtains for conference rooms
7. DJ's for events

I'd collected at *other* meetings, scratched out the names, and wrote mine on them—this is what I handed out. The idea I was trying to convey was that if I was cheap enough to repurpose business cards, I clearly wouldn't be spending

⑧ Caterers for company lunches and meetings
⑨ Our office space,
⑩ Computer repair
⑪ Graphic designers
⑫ A giant Bounce-E-Bounce for a Fun Friday activity
⑬ A "laughter yoga" instructor
⑭ hundreds of manequin legs used to display the wrap boot in retail spaces at launch

money needlessly. And the cards I used were all from very important people I'd met in the entertainment world, so the cards also showed prospective investors that I was meeting their competitors.

REWARD EMPLOYEES

In the early days, you might not be able to pay people well—if at all—but if you feed them well, you'll have a happy staff. Interns with full stomachs are happy and productive—and they value the gesture. At TOMS, therefore, we've always served good food; for interns and kids just out of college, a great barbecue or Tex-Mex lunch is a big deal and a sign that even if they're working for little money, they're appreciated.

We would also get creative with gifts and prizes. For example, every Friday at two o'clock we used to stop working to hold our weekly outdoor bocce-ball tournament. I put up $150 as a prize for the winning team, and the game would turn into a fierce competition; when it got dark outside, we turned on car headlights to illuminate the backyard.

Because I love tea so much, other businesspeople tend to send me large quantities of it—far too much for me to drink. So I make sure everyone at TOMS has lots of tea available, all the time. They also have plenty of outfits to choose from, because people send me closetfuls of clothes, hoping TOMS will use them in a photo shoot. Several times a year we hold a "Blake's Garage Sale," in which everything is free for the taking; everyone takes a number, and even those among the last to choose get to walk off with something.

As a reward for working so hard, the entire TOMS family goes on a ski trip to Mammoth Mountain each year.

Similarly, when I moved onto my sailboat a few years ago, I cleared out most of my material possessions, including clothes, and offered them to my employees. My style tends to be very distinctive: plaid pants, funny shirts, outrageous jackets. People took as much as they could, and for the next year I'd randomly see many of the men in the office dressed exactly as I did. To a stranger, it could have looked like TOMS had a mandatory uniform of funny plaid pants.

THE AGE OF FREE

There are also a myriad of free tools out there to help you with everything from Web development to public relations. Here are some that I've used productively and strongly recommend:*

- Read *The 4-Hour Workweek* by Tim Ferriss (free at the library!); it has excellent practical information on stretching your resources.

- Check out Lifehacker.com. The blog has tons of tips and tricks for increasing your productivity.

- Read Seth Godin's blog, www.sethgodin.typepad .com. One of my marketing mentors, Seth is full of innovative ideas for using new media and other accessible, guerrilla techniques for marketing your work.

- Boost your serendipity by using Twitter. When it comes to getting a job or discovering new things, you might be surprised to learn how much you can gain

---

* You can find an updated version of this list at www.StartSomethingThatMatters .com.

by following friends of friends on Twitter. Our immediate friends already go to the same parties we do, know the same people, and listen to the same music. Not so with our weaker links (friends of friends of friends), who can turn us on to new things.

- Compete (www.compete.com) and Quantcast (www.quantcast.com) can tell you how many monthly visitors your competitors' websites are getting and the search terms that are generating the most traffic for them. If you know what's working for your competitors, you can make it work for you too.

- Similarly, SpyFu (www.spyfu.com) can help you find out competitors' online advertising spending, plus keyword and ad-word details. If their strategies are working, it's likely they'll work for you too.

- Book trips through Kayak (www.kayak.com), the easiest site on which to find and buy plane tickets, car rentals, and hotel reservations. Kayak aggregates other travel search engines like Orbitz.com and CheapTickets.com, saving you both time and money. Another great new site in this space: www.hipmunk.com.

- Do Doodle (www.doodle.com): This is a great tool for setting up meetings with multiple people who have busy schedules. Send a link with proposed times and dates to the people you need to meet; check back later and Doodle will tell you the ones that work for the most people.

- Check out Project Gutenberg (www.gutenberg.org), a digital library of more than 30,000 free eBooks to read on your computer or PDA.

- Tap LibriVox (www.librivox.org), which lets you listen to thousands of audiobooks for free.

- Look into iStockphoto (www.istockphoto.com), the Net's largest source of royalty-free photos, vector illustrations, videos, and Flash files.

- View Footage Firm (www.footagefirm.com), a great source of free and low-cost royalty-free stock video footage.

- With FreeConferenceCall.com, you can get a free, personalized conference-call number. The service offers inexpensive international numbers as well.

- Try LegalZoom (www.legalzoom.com), an inexpensive resource providing documents for company formation, trademarks, patents, copyrights, and other legal issues.

- Access Weebly (www.weebly.com), a platform similar to WordPress that allows you to quickly and easily

---

THE CHELSEA INN

Whenever I have to spend a night in New York City, I stay at what I call the Chelsea Inn. This is my friend Rachel Shechtman's couch in her Manhattan apartment. Over the years, the Chelsea Inn has saved the company tens of thousands of dollars—and it lets me reconnect with a good friend as well.

create websites, even if you have no HTML experience.

- Participate at 99designs (www.99designs.com), which
  provides a very inexpensive way to get logos, business
  cards, and websites designed. The service is based on
  a contest system in which you fill out a simple form
  about what you're looking to design (e.g., "I want to
  create a logo for my company, with XYZ specifica-
  tions") and set a budget for what you're willing to
  pay. Designers from around the world then submit
  concepts based on your requirements. As designs are
  being submitted, you rate the ones that you like the
  best and give feedback on how the designs can be
  improved. After a set amount of time (usually seven
  days), you choose the winning design and pay the designer the prize amount.

As you can see, TOMS takes resourcefulness seriously.
It's a habit successful enterprises never lose. Earmark this
part of the book, and I promise you will go back to it over
and over again as you go forward with your plan.

five

Keep it simple

In character, in manner, in style, in all things, the supreme excellence is simplicity.

—HENRY WADSWORTH LONGFELLOW

Michele Sipolt Kapustka loves the mail. Michele, the middle child of five kids, still lives in the same blue-collar Chicago neighborhood where she grew up, is married to her high school sweetheart, and now has a large family (four boys) of her own.

Throughout her life, Michele has loved getting, sending, and working with mail. She fondly remembers the birthday cards she received as a child from her great-aunt Zoe, even though she saw Zoe regularly, because they "made the birthday special." And when she was ten years old and her best friend moved to Florida, she enjoyed writing letters back and forth all the time, making every delivery day potentially special too.

Michele, who worked as a creative director at a direct-mail company for seventeen years, eventually saw her interest in writing letters develop into a passion for mailing *objects*. Wherever she might be, if she saw something she liked, from a sugar packet to chopsticks, she'd think to herself, *Who can I mail this to?* After all, she says, "Lumpy mail is exciting—when you get a stack of mail, isn't the one with something unusual in it the most fun?"

One day in 2000, Michele was in a drugstore, buying a greeting card for a new mom, when she saw a bunch of balls in a bin and decided it would be more fun to send a ball than a card. She bought it, wrote on it "Have a ball with your baby!," and off it went to the post office, with no further packaging. And then, because her friend loved it so much, Michele started sending balls to other friends for other occasions—fun, but not a serious business.

Three years later, Michele was at the post office, mailing yet another ball, when the man behind her in line asked what she was doing. Michele showed him. He loved the idea and asked if she would do the same for him. She said, "Hey, it's easy—just run on over to the drugstore, pick up a ball, grab a Sharpie, write a message, come back here, and mail it."

But he wanted her to do it for him. She said no. He pleaded. She declined. Finally he offered, "I'll give you five dollars." She consented.

"Lady," he said, "you're selling yourself short. I would have given you twice that."

She smiled. Bingo!

Michele immediately called her sister Melisa, who said, "Mich, we are really onto something here." Melisa went online and bought a website, www.SENDaBALL.com, and a business was born.

Michele and Melisa live across the street from each other, and for years they had been trying to figure out a way to allow at least one of them to stay home with the kids (they have seven between them). Now they had a home-based business that would let them do that. Their brother Marc offered to help as well, and soon they were sending balls all over the world and making a living with their new company. In 2010, SENDaBALL shipped over 20,000 balls—in 2011, it will be 25,000 to 30,000 and they will break a million dollars in total sales.

The SENDaBALL sisters received constant offers and advice from people suggesting ways to expand, change, or grow—even how to develop a manufacturing arm. But Michele's philosophy for the business is based on baby steps: "I can't take those giant leaps. I don't want to branch out. I just want to make this simple idea better."

The only change SENDaBALL has made has been to expand into the corporate business marketplace, sending out custom balls to mailing lists. In the meantime, the business remains pure and simple: an order, a ball, a Sharpie, and a couple of stamps.

In fact, Michele still writes some of the messages on the

balls herself. "It's not complicated. You have to have good handwriting and a sense of humor. That's it."

S implicity is simple.
Perhaps this sounds redundant. But it's true, and it's important. If you're searching for success—whether you're starting a business, already working in one, or thinking about switching to a new career—think simple. Businesses like Michele's SENDaBALL long ago realized this wisdom and have used simplicity to make both waves and money.

At TOMS, this philosophy guides two primary areas: simplicity of product design and simplicity of business model. The latter value applies to all businesses. The former pertains only to businesses that are design-oriented. If your business is a service, there are ways to keep your service simple as well. More about that later.

STRIP IT DOWN

Let's start with design: TOMS' design is based on a shoe, the Argentinian *alpargata*, that has been around for more than one hundred years. The shoe's straightforward, comfortable design makes it an easy fit for everyone: It's a piece of canvas draped around the foot and attached to a sole. It looks good, it's easy to slip on and off, and it dries quickly, which is important for the Argentinian farmers who have to deal with sudden summer showers in their fields.

To create TOMS, we translated that basic design into

an American version by creating a more durable sole and in-sole. But at all costs we preserved the shoe's basic simplicity.

Look how well other shoe brands in the same cat-egory have successfully relied on a simple, traditional de-

Style Your Sole parties have always been an easy and fun way to spread the TOMS story.

sign: UGGs are based on a simple sheepskin boot used by sheep farmers in Australia; Havaiana flip-flops are based on brightly colored rubber shoes from Brazil. Both types of footwear are the essence of simplicity, and both have become cool and popular with urban customers.

For TOMS, there are many advantages to simplicity of design. For one thing, we use the basic shoe as a blank canvas, which has allowed us to create many great designs and special limited editions with celebrity partners such as Hanson, the Dave Matthews Band, Brandon Boyd (lead singer of the band Incubus), and actress Charlize Theron. The simple design has also allowed us to launch the Style Your Sole (SYS) program, which is very popular among TOMS fans on high school and college campuses. SYS parties are events at which TOMS fans get together and decorate shoes with paint, markers, or anything else they want. Many of our retail events involve an SYS component. The TOMS shoe also lends itself to another creative audience—little kids! Thousands of kids now hold birthday parties at which they color and decorate tiny TOMS with their friends; their parents love it because it's not just engaging, creative play for their kids; the experience also offers a lesson in giving to others.

n design, simplicity rules. Look at the world around you—many of the most successful design concepts are also the simplest. The most obvious and ubiquitous examples can be found in Apple's product line, and specifically the iPod. When it was introduced, the small music player wasn't the first of its kind, and it lacked some of the features offered by its competition, like a radio receiver. It's also comparatively expensive, and its battery system is harder to replace than that of its rivals.

But the iPod has something the others don't have: simplicity of design and ease of use. No product looks cleaner and is less complicated to operate. This has always been Apple's forte: creating straightforward designs that even people who are timid with technology can embrace. By 2010, nine years after the iPod was launched, Apple had sold 250 million units—many to people who never dreamed they could so easily master the art of storing and listening to all their music in such a minimal device.

Another example of expertly used simplicity: Google. Here's a story from the business biography *Inside Larry and Sergey's Brain*, by Richard L. Brandt. Marissa Mayer, Google's vice president of search products and user experience, once received an unusual response from someone following her blog. It was simply the number 37. Mayer didn't know what this meant, so she went through her email history to see if the person had sent other messages. He had—nothing but single numbers: 33, 53, and then one that said: "61, getting a bit heavy, aren't we?" There was also a comment: "What happened to the days of 13?"

Marissa soon realized that the emails were appearing on the day she launched changes on Google's home page, and the numerals referred to the number of words on the page. She had thought she was keeping the page simple, but it didn't occur to her to count the words on it—which is now her standard procedure. At this time, the company won't allow more than twenty-eight.

A SIMPLE OPERATION

Simplicity can apply to an idea, a goal, or a mission, as in the case of Surgeons OverSeas (SOS), founded by thirty-five-year-old Dr. Peter Kingham and forty-five-year-old Dr. Adam Kushner.

Both Peter and Adam grew up in the New York City area, Peter in Larchmont and Adam in Manhattan. Peter studied the history of medicine at Yale, and while in medical school at SUNY Stonybrook, he volunteered in a medical clinic in rural Tanzania. Later, as a surgical resident at New York University Medical Center, he worked in Malawi as a Yale/Stanford Johnson and Johnson international health scholar. Today he is an attending surgeon in the Division of Hepatopancreatobiliary Surgery at New York's Memorial Sloan-Kettering Cancer Center.

Adam, the son of a physician, studied history at Cornell University. His interest in trauma surgery crystallized a month before medical school when, in Yugoslavia at the start of the Bosnian War, he watched helplessly as his guide died from a gunshot wound.

Having met while doing medical work in developing countries, Peter and Adam realized they shared a goal: to help local surgeons develop the skills they needed to save lives. With SOS, they made that goal the core value of their organization. Instead of importing teams of surgeons, anesthesiologists, and nurses, or teaming up with vast global medical organizations, SOS focuses on streamlining medical processes and empowering local surgeons to act independently of outside help.

This is how Peter and Adam describe their mission: "As surgeons, we know how good it feels to go to developing countries and do a large number of operations, but we realized that if we could teach local surgeons, or even help local surgeons teach junior doctors in their own country, we could really make a difference. The local surgeons are the experts. We can assist with teaching material, supplies, and moral support, but for the long term it is up to them. It's their country after all; shouldn't they have the skills to care for their own population?" That's SOS's constant and simple focus, from which it never strays.

Simplicity of mission helps your customers focus on the true value you provide. Take the case of In-N-Out Burger. This privately held hamburger chain, founded in 1948 by Harry and Esther Snyder, now has almost 250 stores across the western United States. The Snyders' plan was always simple: "Give customers the freshest, highest-quality foods you can buy and provide them with friendly service in a sparkling clean environment." That's all they've done for more than six decades.

There aren't many choices at In-N-Out: Basically, you order a burger and fries and a beverage. There's nothing complicated, including the décor, as every store is colored in basic red, white, and yellow. And yet In-N-Out was one of only a few restaurant chains mentioned positively by author

Eric Schlosser in his bestselling exposé of fast-food chains, *Fast Food Nation;* Schlosser praised In-N-Out for using natural, fresh ingredients, as well as for treating its employees well.

"Keep it real simple. Do one thing and do it the best you can," says Harry Snyder.

Simple ideas are also easily adaptable to changing times—and sometimes they never have to be adapted at all. One hundred forty years ago, a Nevada tailor named Jacob Davis wrote a letter to a wealthy San Francisco businessman, offering his unusual but potentially profitable idea for improving the quality of workers' pants. The merchant to whom Davis wrote had emigrated from Bavaria to New York City and then headed for San Francisco to seek his fortune in the Gold Rush. Instead of panning for gold, however, the young immigrant started a dry-goods business that imported clothing, umbrellas, handkerchiefs, and bolts of fabric to be sold to merchants, including Davis, all along the West Coast.

When many of his customers complained that their pants were falling apart, Davis had come up with the simple idea that sewing metal rivets at the pockets' stress points would create durability—but he didn't have the sixty-eight dollars it would cost to file for a patent, so he reached out to the young immigrant-turned-businessman and asked if he might want to work with him. The businessman was enthusiastic about the idea, and on May 20, 1873, a patent was granted. These rivet-reinforced pants, in fundamentally the same design, are still popular today. Jacob Davis's partner was Levi Strauss.

Here are some more simple ideas that have become great companies:

CHIPOTLE: After graduating from culinary school in 1990, twenty-five-year-old Steve Ells moved to San Francisco and frequented the taco and burrito joints that had sprung up in the city's Mission District. Ells's idea: Create a high-quality Mexican-food experience using organic ingredients and naturally raised meat while keeping the menu as simple as possible and using assembly-line techniques for speedy service. In 1993, with a loan from his father, Ells opened the first Chipotle in Colorado. Today there are more than 1,000 Chipotle restaurants in thirty-eight states, Canada, and the United Kingdom. In 2010, their net income was $178 million and they employed 26,500 people.

CRAIGSLIST: While working as a computer-security architect, forty-three-year-old Craig Newmark started a small email list to keep friends updated on local art and technology events in San Francisco. His subscriber base increased rapidly, and in 1996, Newmark decided to create a free website, called craigslist, that closely modeled the typical classified ads in newspapers. It became an instant hit. Today craigslist has expanded to more than 700 cities in seventy countries around the world, and it is the seventh-most-trafficked website in the United States.

DAILYCANDY: Frustrated with the agonizingly slow pace of magazines, in 2000 writer Dany Levy decided to create an email newsletter featuring style and fashion tips, dining recommendations, and cool events happening in New York City. She called her newsletter "DailyCandy" and sent it off to about 700 friends, family members, and people she considered influential. The tone of the emails was light and fun, and it worked: Today, DailyCandy editions are sent out in Atlanta, Boston, Chicago, Dallas, London, Los Angeles, Philadelphia, Miami, San Francisco, Seattle, and Washington, D.C. In 2008, Comcast purchased DailyCandy for $125 million.

DONORSCHOOSE: In 2000, twenty-five-year-old Charles Best was working as a social studies teacher in the Bronx. Frustrated by the lack of resources in public schools, Best sensed that people wanted to donate to education—but wanted a way to connect directly with individual classrooms. So he invented the website DonorsChoose.org. There, public-school teachers make requests for specific items they need for their classrooms, from pencils to musical instruments, and donors browse the requests and give any amount that inspires them. All donors receive a thank-you note from the teacher making the request, photos of the ongoing project, and a report showing how the money was spent. As of this writing, DonorsChoose has raised more than $73 million and helped more than three million students in 35,000 public schools across the country.

HEIFER INTERNATIONAL: Heifer International's simple idea: Livestock has the power to lift families out of the poverty cycle. The organization was first conceived in 1939 when

relief worker Dan West, rationing powdered milk to refugees of the Spanish Civil War, realized that handouts would
never be enough—poor families needed animals to plow
their fields, to produce milk and eggs they could use to feed
their children, and to leave behind manure they could use to
improve the quality of their soil. Today, Heifer International
gives livestock from goats to water buffalo to rural families
in more than 125 countries.

Heifer also teaches the importance of planting trees,
collecting manure for organic fertilizer, preventing over-
grazing, and planning for long-term success. Recipients take
part in the giving cycle by agreeing to share one or more of
their animals' offspring with others; Heifer calls this "Pass-
ing on the Gift."

NETFLIX: After selling his software-engineering company
in 1997, thirty-seven-year-old entrepreneur Reed Hastings turned his attention to an entirely different business:
DVD rentals. At the time, people were accustomed to going
to Blockbuster or a local video store to pick up their VHS
tapes. Hastings's simple idea: Put DVDs in the mail and
send them directly to people's homes. Today Netflix offers
more than 100,000 titles online and has ten million monthly
subscribers. Back in 2007, the company announced its one
billionth DVD delivery. Wow!

SOUTHWEST AIRLINES: In 1966, Texas entrepreneur Rol-
lin King showed his lawyer, Herb Kelleher, a triangle he'd
drawn on a cocktail napkin. The triangle represented the

state of Texas; on each point, King wrote the name of a city: Dallas, Houston, and San Antonio. At the time, flying between these cities was inconvenient and expensive; King wanted to create a low-cost intrastate airline servicing this Texan triangle. Kelleher liked the idea. Today the company he founded, Southwest Airlines, carries more passengers per year than any other airline and posts a profit every year. The secret? They keep things simple by making Southwest the absolutely cheapest option for passengers on short-distance flights. Kelleher, who stepped down as CEO in 2008, once said, "I can teach you the secret to running this airline in thirty seconds. This is it: We are *the* low-fare airline. Once you understand that fact, you can make any decision about this company's future as well as I can."

UNCLUTTER YOUR WORK SPACE

Many who opt for simplicity in their business model also seek it in their business space. Personally, I am more creative when I'm not surrounded by a lot of stuff. That's why I have some of my best ideas on airplanes, where there are no distracting gadgets, emails, or phone calls. This is also why TOMS' current work space is essentially a warehouse with no offices. Every employee has a plywood workstation that resembles a small cube, and because the cubes are only four and a half feet tall, they're as easy to talk over as a backyard fence. This setup encourages easy and quick communication—anyone can talk to anyone else at any time; there is little division between the top executives and the customer-service people. If someone has a question, they just stand up and ask. As we are in the process of building our next headquarters, we are keeping this kind of open arrangement.

As mentioned in Chapter 4, you don't need bells and whistles to run a business. All you really need is a website, business cards, and a place where you can work. Outside of that, you can meet at Starbucks, you can get office help from FedEx Office, you can use the postal facilities at Mail Boxes Etc., you can hire an answering service, and you can rent a by-the-hour conference room.

Many companies, small and large, have adopted the simple model. For example, Netflix no longer has vacation or sick policies, because keeping track of all this data was expensive and overtaxed the human-resources department.

The office has changed a lot . . . but we're still true to our humble roots.

If a company has the right employees, they won't take advantage of paid days off—they'll leave only when it makes the most sense for them to do so.

Semco is a fast-growing company in Brazil that manufactures everything from boat pumps and industrial-strength dishwashers to mixers and scales. Its CEO, Ricardo Semler, has created the simplest of work environments: He took down all office walls, removed dress codes, and eliminated time cards. Even simpler, he allows employees themselves to decide which managers they want to work for and to set their own salaries (which are then posted publicly). This simplicity has helped the company grow from a $4-million business to a $200-million one since Ricardo took over the reins.

Costco is another company with a simplicity-minded leader. CEO Jim Sinegal believes that if his company is supposed to stand for savings and simplicity, so should he. At the company's headquarters in Washington, Sinegal's desk is an ordinary table that he bought from a used-furniture store more than twenty-five years ago. Much of the other furniture in the office is left over from the company that owned the building before Costco.

The easier it is for someone to understand who you are and what you stand for, the easier it will be for that person to spread the word to others. Having a clear function, design, and purpose means that your story can be spread easily, whether you're pitching it to investors or chatting to riders in elevators. Someone must understand it before they can adopt it or purchase it. It's really that simple.

Keeping it simple means the message is also sticky. When people hear a catchy phrase or idea, it stays in their head and they tell others. That's why so many of the greatest taglines and mantras in the corporate world have been the most direct. You are constantly being bombarded by messages from companies wanting your attention and your business. The more straightforward that message, the more likely it is to penetrate your filters.

You don't have to wait to start a business to enjoy simplicity. I've found that simplicity in life can be as important as it is in business.

Early on in TOMS' Shoe Drops, I (like countless others before) noticed that the people we met who seemed the happiest were most often those who possessed the least. The kids in the rural areas we visited, who owned little, often radiated a kind of joy about life that we saw far less frequently in the urban areas. The more I thought about this, the more obvious it seemed: Complicated lives and heaps of possessions don't necessarily bring happiness; in fact, they can bring the opposite.

After that revelation, I decided to get rid of most of my belongings and move onto a sailboat. At the time, I was living in a nice loft in Venice, a typical bachelor pad featuring a huge television, fancy entertainment system, cool furniture, gourmet kitchen with two stoves, special refrigerator to keep wine at the perfect temperature, and artwork on all the walls; it was filled with cameras, clothes, shoes, and all the other junk we human beings collect. The more I looked around, the more I saw that I owned far too much stuff, little of which I really needed.

When I moved onto a 200-square-foot sailboat, I had no room for these belongings. So I divested myself, selling and giving away almost everything, keeping only sporting equipment and the books I loved. (One day, when I own a house, I'll keep a full library of books. Books are different from other possessions—they're more like friends.)

Once I got rid of all those things, I felt remarkably free. That led to greater peace of mind and, from a business standpoint, more creativity. Without clutter, I think more clearly than I ever have.

The move to the boat was my catalyst for simplicity.

One of my favorite photos from the first Shoe Drop in Argentina.

Now ask yourself: How much do *you* really need in life? How many clothes? How many toys? Look around you. Maybe before you can come up with the simple idea that's going to be your next step in business, you need to create a simple environment in which to live and work.

ere are a few starter tips:

KEEP A NOTEBOOK—ELECTRONIC OR PAPER—WITH YOU AT ALL TIMES

There's so much to keep track of, and the mind can retain only so many things. Rather than trust that I'll remember something and add it to the clutter of information already floating through my mind, I write down everything that's important, whether it's the name of someone I want to meet or a sudden idea for a new design. When you write things down, you let your mind off the hook, giving it more room for things like problem-solving or spontaneous creativity.

OWN AS LITTLE AS YOU CAN GET AWAY WITH

Seriously—how much do you need? The fact is, the more you have, the more effort and money you have to spend taking care of it, which distracts you from enjoying it. People tend to buy lots of luxury goods, thinking it will give them a better lifestyle, but what they really create is a drain for their time and energy as well as their savings.

The best way to get around not owning much is to rent whenever possible. If you enjoy sailing and go ten times a year, don't buy a boat. If you drive only now and then, rent a car or join a car-share service. When you rent rather than own, you reduce the need for maintenance and the headache of taking care of pricey objects.

SCHEDULE EVERYTHING

It sounds counterintuitive, but scheduling actually simplifies life and allows you to let go of worry. People often ask me if having a full schedule is stressful. In the past I was often preoccupied with trying to make time to see friends or returning phone calls. Now I schedule everything, so that when I'm with a person, I am totally present. I don't check to see if I need to talk to someone else.

COMBINE!

I love being near the water and I love sailing, and that's why, when I moved out of my loft and needed a place to live, I bought a sailboat and moved onto it full time. (If I didn't live on it, of course, I would have considered renting one.) Three

goals—being near water, sailing, and finding a new home—
were accomplished with one act. Similarly, I like being phys-
ically fit, but I don't have a lot of time to exercise, so I ride
my bike to work whenever I can, getting my workout on my
way to the office. And by pedaling instead of driving, I'm
being earth-friendly, another one of my objectives.

DON'T LET TECHNOLOGY ENSLAVE YOU

Too many people take what's good about technology—the
convenience—and turn it into a form of oppression. For me,
the BlackBerry or iPhone is a great simplifier; it allows me
to work from anywhere in the world, but I use it with purpose: i.e., I don't let it control me. I use it when necessary,
not through habit.

One way I do this is by having a private email account
as well as a business one. Try it—and remember not to look
at the latter on weekends. I tell my staff that I don't want to
hear from them on weekends, and I do my best to save my
ideas in draft form so I don't interrupt theirs either.

CLEAN UP

Clean out your closet. Clean out your storage drawers—at
least four times a year. I firmly believe that the less stuff
you have sitting around, the less stuff you have cluttering up
your mind.

THE SIMPLE PLAN

Write *one* sentence to answer the questions below that pertain to what you are trying to do. For some of you, that could be all of them; for others, it might be just one:

TIM FERRISS'S TIPS ON SIMPLICITY

Since my friend Tim Ferriss is an expert on time management, I asked him to offer some tips on how to master simplicity in your life. Here's what he had to say:

First, on the bright side, most people are rediscovering that, even if a 401k or salary drops 30 percent, the most important things are actually the easiest to obtain: great friends, good food, and a decent bottle of wine. They are, in effect, living philosopher Seneca's advice: "Set aside a certain number of days, during which you shall be content with the scantiest and cheapest fare, with coarse and rough dress, saying to yourself the while: 'Is this the condition that I feared?'"

Put another way, it's better to design an ideal lifestyle and then fill in the gaps with high-output streamlined work than to fill the calendar with as much as possible and hope an acceptable lifestyle will be the by-product. Based on more than 1,000 case studies on my blog (www .fourhourblog.com) and elsewhere, it's clear the latter just doesn't work.

Here are several tactics to help keep things simple, uncluttered, and high-impact:

1) Do an 80/20 analysis of how you spend your time and create a "not-to-do" list

What are the 20 percent of activities and distractions/interruptions that consume 80 percent of your time? Use a program like www.rescuetime .com if you must, but figure out what's eating your usable time. Then write the top two to four distractions/interruptions on a not-to-do list and review them each morning, attempting for just one to two days to stop doing them. Consider using Rescue-Time to block sites like Facebook and Twitter during certain hours.

1) What is your business about?
2) What do you want to be known for as a person?
3) Why should someone hire you?
4) What social cause are you seeking to serve?
5) If you are designing a product or a service, look at it and

2) Experiment with a low-cost virtual assistant (VA)

What would you do if you had three-day weekends for the rest of your life? If you can save just eight hours per week with a VA, that's effectively what you've done. It's well possible for most people to remove ten to forty hours per week within two months this way. It gives you the breathing room not only to pursue dreams otherwise postponed until retirement but also to focus on high-yield, revenue-generating activities versus administration and personal chores. It is a fundamental lifestyle upgrade and an eye-opening experience. Once you try it, you will never go back to how things used to be. Check out www.tryasksunday.com, www.elance.com (search "virtual assistant"), or even the refugees of www.samasource.org to get a taste of the options. If you prefer U.S.-based help, take a look at www.redbutler.com.

3) Don't check email until 11 a.m.

Focus on completing your most uncomfortable "to-do" before that time.

4) Learn to let the small bad things happen

Many people have accepted and made peace with letting little bad things happen to get the big important things done—for example, returning a phone call a bit late and apologizing, paying a small late fee for returning "X" (books, DVDs, whatever), or losing an unreasonable customer. The answer to being overwhelmed is not spinning more plates—or doing more—it's defining the few things that can fundamentally change your business and life. Then you can allow yourself to let the smaller things slide.

Think of the small, reversible (or just unimportant) bad things as your productivity tax. Parking ticket? Irking that high-maintenance "friend" who sucks the life out of you? Focus on the critical few, not the trivial many.

then decide: What else can you remove from the design or service and still keep its function intact?

The key is to answer the appropriate questions using a single sentence. If you can't, then consider going back to the drawing board until you've honed your answers down to a simple statement.

six

build trust

He who does not trust enough will not be trusted.
—LAO-TZU

Over the last two decades, Tony Hsieh, the son of Taiwanese immigrants, has been one of the most successful entrepreneurs in America. His first business, founded in 1996 when he was twenty-two years old, was Link Exchange, an Internet advertising company that, at its peak, reached more than 50 percent of all Internet-enabled households every month. He and his partners sold the company to Microsoft in 1999 for $265 million.

That same year, Tony joined the start-up Zappos, the online retail giant. By 2008, Zappos was grossing more than $1 billion in merchandise sales (and is continuing to grow). A year later, it was bought by Amazon.com for an approximate valuation of $1.2 billion on closing day.

As part of the Amazon deal, Tony and his team vowed to stay on at Zappos and continue not just to grow the company but to nourish its culture as well. Zappos has built a reputation as one of the country's best places to work (it ranked among the top fifteen in *Fortune* magazine's 2010 "Best Companies to Work For") and to shop (its customer satisfaction is extremely high; on any given day, 75 percent of its orders come from repeat customers).

Tony has shared with me many of the secrets to his success, but one of the most important is the highly respected culture he created at Zappos, a culture that, at its core, relies on trust. "Trust is a fundamental part of a business," Tony says. "It's the most important part of getting our work done right. A brand succeeds or fails based on whether or not people trust the company with which they're about to do business."

That trust works on various levels and includes employees, vendors, and customers. For example, according to Tony, "Organizations can only function at peak capacity if their employees are looking out for the best interests of the company, not just motivated by their own selfish reasons."

To further trust, Tony encourages his employees to get to know one another as friends and to spend time together outside the office. By building high levels of trust through their personal interactions, they can establish communications that work well inside and outside the company. "People are more likely to do favors for each other if they are friends, not just co-workers," he says.

Another way Zappos builds trust among its internal and external partners is to mean exactly what it says. "The other day I sent out a blog post updating the situation on the one-year anniversary of our acquisition by Amazon. When the acquisition first occurred, I wrote a long memo to the staff, covering every point I could think of to make it clear exactly what was happening and why this acquisition was a great moment. In my blog, I followed up on every point in that letter, showing what was promised and planned and what actually happened. For example, we'd vowed we would remain independent and maintain the Zappos brand. Plenty of naysayers said they had heard this kind of stuff before and that it was never true, that the acquired company always gets swallowed up. That may indeed be true for most acquisitions, but Zappos still has its independence, and that letter I wrote a year ago still stands."

Unlike many companies, Zappos actively encourages its employees to join its aggregated Twitter account and to Tweet whatever they wish. Whereas other companies police their employees' words, Zappos tells its employees to use their best judgment, and that's it.

And then there are the programs for which Zappos has become famous, the best-known being its custom of giving $3,000 to any prospective employee who takes the company training but decides not to take a job. Zappos wants committed employees. Approximately 98 percent of trainees refuse the quick-cash offer and join the company.

Another quirky program: Zappos lets employees give anyone else in the company a fifty-dollar bonus if they feel that person deserves it, up to one bonus a month.

As a result of this trust, Zappos employees tend to stay. The turnover rates vary by department, but all in all they are far lower than those of Zappos' competitors.

Zappos also works to ensure trust with its vendors and customers. The company deals with more than 1,500 brands, but none get lost in the shuffle; all are treated with a personal touch. "We don't see a business relationship as being just business. Trust is something you build in all aspects of all relationships," Tony says.

"Traditionally there's been an adversarial relationship between the retailer and the wholesaler. This is because it usually plays out as a zero-sum game: There's a limited amount of money to be shared between the two, and every penny the retailer makes is one the wholesaler loses, and vice versa. Since we look at our vendors as partners, our goal is to build a business that makes sense for both companies in the long term. If you trust each other, you can build a business relationship bigger than the sum of its parts."

Trust is Zappos' default way of thinking. Other companies may earn trust, but at Zappos trust is built in from the beginning. "And, yes, sometimes we do have to deal with untrustworthy people, but it's been so rare it hasn't caused anyone to doubt our general policy," Tony says.

Trust is an enormous subject, but I want to boil it down to two fundamental aspects: 1) the internal trust you build within an organization as a leader and 2) the external trust you build with your customers, your vendors, and your donors (if you're a nonprofit).

INTERNAL TRUST

Between the birth of the Industrial Revolution and the modern workplace, a wide chasm formed between employer and employee. Frederick W. Taylor, whose book *The Principles of Scientific Management* was the bible for the industrial age, applied so-called scientific analysis to improving workplace productivity. Fundamental to his theory were the following ideas: Workers are inherently lazy and do not enjoy their jobs. Managers should break down work into the smallest possible tasks and supervise and control everything their workforce does. Workers should be paid according to their performance over a set amount of time. Workers are most productive when driven by monetary incentives.

A business organized by Taylorite principles sent a clear message to its workers: You are not ever going to be trusted with any significant responsibility. And you shouldn't trust your employer to do anything beyond pay you for the hours you've clocked in.

Not all employers ruled like this, and not all employees felt alienated and dehumanized by the companies they worked for. But it's safe to say that, in general, the word "trust" was not baked into the operating DNA of business leadership during this period.

I cannot think of any area of business during the past

few decades in which the mindset of successful leaders has changed so much. Today, trust between employer and employee is the cornerstone of your business and your future.

As a leader, your job is to motivate your staff, your co-workers, and your partners—anyone you're in a position to influence and direct. Whereas past leaders tended to be egomaniacal and charismatic, commanders in the mode of a General Patton, these days great leaders are those who trust and empower their staff. After all, we all derive enormous satisfaction from feeling that we're in control of our jobs rather than being victims of them—and, as a leader, that's not a difficult feeling to provide.

Always remember: The better your employees feel about their jobs, the better your business performs. One way to motivate is to make sure your team is all on the same page, or, as one of my mentors, Lou George, says, "that we are all hearing stereo." When the team is working together and hearing the same direction, their confidence soars.

Although many reasons exist for the recent shift from authoritarianism to trust, a leading factor is the way that knowledge moves through the workforce. It used to be that information traveled vertically, from the top down: The important ideas and information were generated in the executive offices at headquarters and then filtered, selectively, to employees.

The contemporary workplace is much flatter: A company can enjoy valuable contributions from all levels of employees at all locations, whether they're interns, part-timers, or executives, and whether they're based in Chicago, Shanghai, or the Shetland Islands. There's no telling where the next great idea will come from and how it will move through the organization—top down, bottom up, or zigzagging through the middle.

For good ideas to flow smoothly, your people have to first feel empowered to offer—and execute—them. You can't motivate someone by giving him or her the position but not the power to do the job or to voice input. Powerlessness is the ultimate demotivator.

Among the modern leaders who turned the tide away from the Taylor management model is Bill Hewlett, co-founder of computer giant Hewlett-Packard. As recounted in the book *The Speed of Trust* by Stephen M. R. Covey, Stephen R. Covey, and Rebecca R. Merrill, one weekend Hewlett went to a company storeroom, searching for a tool, and discovered a lock on the tool bin. HP had always allowed employees open access to all tools, a decision made to show how much the company trusted its workforce. Hewlett broke open the lock and put up a sign: "HP Trusts Its Employees."

Packard was later quoted as saying, "The open bins and storerooms were a symbol of trust, a trust that is central to the way HP does business."

A phrase that has gained much traction over the last four decades is "servant leadership." Coined by writer and business consultant Robert K. Greenleaf in his 1970 essay "The Servant as Leader," the term refers to someone who uses qualities like empathy, listening skills, stewardship, and awareness rather than power to assert his or her authority to lead.

Certainly leaders of the past offered this kind of authority; as far back as the fourth century B.C., the Chinese thinker and politician Chanakya wrote that "the leader shall consider as good not what pleases him but what pleases his subjects. . . ." Throughout history, scholars and philosophers from Gandhi to Martin Luther King, Jr., have advocated this kind of guidance.

Recently the concept of the servant leader has enjoyed a surge in popularity, with good reason. Today's successful leaders are those willing to share credit as much as possible, who give away as much as they can, and who promote an environment of creative cooperation instead of rabid competition.

I confess, when I started in business more than a decade ago, my goal was to become a rock-star business leader, someone whose name would resonate throughout the world, someone whose fame would supersede that of others of my generation—the typical cult CEO. But the more I learned about business and, along the way, about the world, the more that urge dissipated. In its place rose the desire to lead with a softer, more human touch. I don't want TOMS to be only about me—everyone in the organization must feel attached to TOMS to the degree that anyone can be a spokesperson whenever it's appropriate.

A leader can create a company, but a community creates a movement.

Truly great servant leaders are inspiring. They create loyal employees who are attached to the company and its mission rather than only to their own careers. Servant leaders realize that their primary job isn't about figuring out what they can get done and cross off their to-do list, but how many people they can help get things crossed off their own to-do lists. It's about making sure that everyone on the team is performing to their fullest capabilities.

So, as a leader, your job is to help others do their jobs better. This is why I tell my top people to help serve everyone in their group.

For example, two of the major executives at TOMS are both quintessential servant leaders—Candice Wolfswinkel, our Shoe Glue, and Jill DiIorio, who runs TOMS' retail sales and marketing in the United States. Interestingly, Candice works in our main office, and Jill operates out of Houston, Texas—almost 1,400 miles away. Both motivate their staffs by inspiring them, recognizing their accomplishments, and letting them get their jobs done as they best see fit. The resulting amount of work is far greater than what either Jill or Candice could have accomplished if they were prioritizing their own tasks instead of enabling their staffs to work better and smarter.

Although there are many aspects to servant leadership, one of the clearest ways to build the kind of trust you'll need to succeed is to admit your own mistakes.

In any endeavor, you (and everyone else) will make them. This is good! Making mistakes can be one of the most important ways for an organization to grow. If you view mistakes not as errors that impede the flow of progress but as opportunities to build more trust in your organization as you work through them, you turn a negative into a positive that will build the trust you'll need.

Certainly I made plenty of mistakes at TOMS. One of the worst was the Airstream shoe debacle.

When TOMS started, we used to travel around in an Airstream trailer, hosting events to raise awareness of our brand and our mission. I love the Airstream brand—it's cool, classic, and stylish, and it stands for an appealing kind of on-the-road freedom. Guessing that other Airstream fans were equally passionate and that they'd love an Airstream shoe from TOMS, I convinced our production team to create 800 pairs, which was a lot for us at the time.

The shoes were beautiful: gray and navy, the Airstream colors, with the image of a U.S. road map as a liner. To promote them, we then decided to have our 2008 sales meeting at the Airstream convention in Perry, Georgia, where 2,000 devotees from all over North America gather every year.

When we arrived at the Airstream convention, it was a remarkable sight to witness all those great people and their wonderful trailers. Of course, most of these intrepid fans were retirees who preferred a nice pair of orthotic shoes over TOMS slip-ons. We had 800 shoes to sell at the convention to a group of people who may have liked the fact that the shoe design echoed the iconic look of an Airstream, or thought the road-map liner was cool, but who didn't want to, or simply couldn't, wear them. We sold five pairs.

When we regrouped in Los Angeles, I came forward and admitted that I'd made a mistake. I'd assumed that what I thought was cool would overpower the demographic dissonance between the average TOMS consumer and the average Airstream enthusiast. It didn't. We decided to commit to some solid research in the future before we made this kind of design decision again.

(By the way, under the heading of "There's a Use for

Everything," the shoes made great gifts to my Airstream-loving friends. And I wore a pair throughout that summer to remind myself to think carefully before jumping.)

As a leader, when you're willing to admit your judgment was poor, you show people that you aren't going to cover your mistakes or place them on someone else. I took 100 percent of the responsibility for my Airstream error. I didn't say that our salespeople didn't work hard enough or that the production people didn't make a good-looking shoe. I didn't say that the research-and-development people had failed. The error in judgment was all mine. I said I had made a mistake. That gained me trust at TOMS. It also gave the rest of the staff a sense that they, too, could make mistakes—it's all part of the learning process.

Since then, whenever someone wants to push an idea through without a lot of solid thinking, we say, "Uh-oh, this could be our next Airstream shoe."

Another mistake I made eventually helped TOMS gain trust outside the company. When we started shipping shoes to major accounts such as Nordstrom, Urban Outfitters, and Active Ride, all of our shoes had a little piece of fabric on the sole—we thought it looked nice, and so did our customers. Once, however, we accidentally created a large batch of shoes—6,000 pairs, to be exact—with too much fabric. When you first put them on, the extra fabric wasn't an issue. But after a few weeks it became well worn, and on a wet day the shoes became far too slippery. People were falling down in the rain.

Our customers didn't complain. But because we knew this was an issue and it bothered us, we went to all our retailers and told them outright about the problem—even though they didn't know about it yet.

TOMS then offered to take back all of the shoes, which was not only a huge financial issue for us but also alerted all of our accounts to a big slipup on our part—and since we were a small company that many of them already doubted, this was a scary move. But our willingness to tell these accounts about our mistake gained us a great deal of trust in the long run. From then on, these retailers knew that TOMS stood behind everything we made.

Conversely, just as you should own up to your mistakes, you must allow room for your employees' lapses as well. They'll misfile claims, or lose orders, or damage goods, or insult a customer. Mistakes happen.

But the cost of the employees' slipups may well be less than the benefit of the personal growth they obtain from them and the value they provide to the organization. If someone in our customer-service department makes a $5,000 mistake, yes, that's money down the drain. But it could also save us a great deal in the future.

Why? Well, for one thing, that person will probably never commit that error again. And, best of all, we don't have to train someone else to do that job—someone who might innocently blunder into that same $5,000 misstep. Now we have someone who is not only experienced but who knows the position's potential pitfalls and is on guard against further mistakes.

It's even possible that some errors are built into the system itself and that someone is bound to make them no matter what. By allowing people to be open about these lapses, you can correct the system.

If you extend more trust than you might normally be comfortable with—and more than most business books tell you to do—even though those mistakes will come with a price, over the long term you'll be paid back with interest.

On the other hand, it's a different matter if the mistake an employee makes involves breaking trust at the company. Here is one area in which you must be ruthless. You must create a culture in which people know there is zero tolerance for breaking trust. Making mistakes, yes. Breaking trust, no.

This next story is highly disguised to protect the innocent and the guilty. At one of my companies I had an employee whom I'll call Jerry, who came to work for us just

MISTAKE OF THE MONTH

There's a Detroit, Michigan, marketing and advertising agency that has taken the valuable lessons learned from making mistakes to a new level: Brogan & Partners gives out a "Mistake of the Month" award to the employee who has committed (and confessed to) the best error. The agency votes on the errors, and the winner gets a cash prize for honesty (sixty dollars). More important, the errors are then publicized throughout the company so that no one will make the same mistake again. Some of the mistakes include putting on a presentation at a client's office without checking to see if the document was intact on the computer (it was a mess) and giving odd gifts to corporate clients. One such gift was a set of three leopard-print golf-club covers, which some clients couldn't identify as such: One person thanked the company for the gift of the mittens but wondered why there were three.

out of college but took to his job as though he had years of experience behind him. He always arrived at the office early, worked long hours, and was a great deal of fun.

However, we soon began to realize that Jerry had a fatal flaw—he loved to gossip. Now, everyone in an office gossips to some degree, and sometimes gossip can actually be good if it's well intentioned or is funny enough to relieve tension. And there's no way any company can, or should, monitor its employees' conversations. But what got back to me and others was that Jerry was actively bad-mouthing people in the company, including members of his team. Anyone whom Jerry didn't like, or anyone with whom he felt competitive, became the object of his funny but mean-spirited gossip. It reached the point where several employees came to me in tears because Jerry had told stories about them that were not only vicious but blatantly untrue.

I have always had a zero-tolerance policy for bad-mouthing other employees. Nothing destroys trust more. So in this case, although Jerry had made a mistake, it was a mistake we could not allow. We fired him.

As painful as it was to fire a competent employee, the end result was an organization where trust grew even more. It made other staffers believe that we do what we say we do—refuse to tolerate anyone who disrupts our culture.

You've got to prune your organization of people who violate company trust. This can be difficult, but it must be done. This goes especially for high-performing employees. In the long run, the success of your company is not based on the two highest-performing employees but on the trust you create within your entire organization. Company culture needs to be maintained at all costs.

EXTERNAL TRUST

Because a major part of leadership takes place outside your organization, you must be sure that you have the trust of your customers, your vendors, and your donors—or whomever you depend upon for your survival. Everything you do in your organization should focus on growing, building, and protecting the trust of these people. If you lose that trust, you lose everything.

The history of American business is filled with examples of companies that destroyed trust with their consumers, from the late telephone giant WorldCom to the retailer Kmart to the oil company BP, which ran ads touting its environmental bona fides but then ended up flooding the Gulf of Mexico with crude oil.

Other companies, when under a trust siege, have responded quickly and intelligently. For example, in 1982, seven Chicago-area residents died when they swallowed cyanide-tainted Tylenol tablets. It was not Tylenol's fault; the tablets were poisoned after Tylenol shipped them to stores. But the police never caught the culprit and, in the hysteria of the moment, people became terrified of the name Tylenol.

Rather than surrender the brand—the market leader in pain-relief medicine—owner Johnson & Johnson did everything it could to restore trust in the product. It spent a fortune alerting customers to the danger, it recalled $100 million worth of product containers, it exchanged already-bought bottles for new ones, it worked with law-enforcement officials on the case, it offered a six-figure reward to help catch the guilty party, and it changed the packaging on the bottles: From then on, all products that could be tampered with were double- or triple-sealed. The strategy worked. Tylenol remains a trusted brand.

Some of the most successful business leaders of the century succeeded precisely because of the trust they created with their customers. Carl Sewell is another of my mentors and is among the most successful entrepreneurs of his era; his book, *Customers for Life*, is still a bestselling classic. In it, and in his life, Carl preaches that trust is one of the most important parts of a business, rather than, say, making money: "For our way of doing business to work, we have to convince you that there is something more valuable than money."

Stores such as Nordstrom are well known for their service, which places customers first. Stories abound at the company of employees who went far out of their way to help customers in ways that no other store would do. As told in *The Nordstrom Way*, by Robert Spector and Patrick McCarthy, a Nordstrom employee once noticed that a customer had left her airline ticket on the counter while shopping at the store; after calling the airline and discovering they wouldn't reissue it, the salesperson left her job for an hour and a half and rushed to the airport, where she had the customer paged and gave her back the ticket. This salesperson was able to decide for herself the best course of action and leave her place at the store—and this is because Nordstrom trusts its workers enough to give them the freedom to make entrepreneurial decisions.

A nother way to build trust is to create a powerful promise for the customer. For example, some companies make money by selling the next generation of their product to replace older, broken ones, but certain brands have built their reputation on a lifetime guarantee. Customers trust this guarantee. Two of my favorite companies that do this well are Tumi, the luggage maker, and Orvis, the fly-fishing outfitter.

One Tumi story I heard involved a customer who called the company about refurbishing his briefcase. The bag had special meaning to him because it was a gift from his father in 1992, and the customer had vowed to use it throughout his entire career; Tumi fixed the old, broken bag with no questions asked. (When the customer sent in the bag, he accidentally left two expensive silver pens in it. When the bag was returned, the pens were still there.)

At Orvis, if you break a fly rod—even if you slam it in your car door—the company will send you a new one. Orvis once replaced a rod whose owner claimed he had broken it while defending himself from a rattlesnake. Another soon-to-be-divorced man returned home to find that his wife had cut all of his fishing rods in half with a saw; he, too, got new ones. In both cases, Orvis asked no questions.

I have been a fly-fisherman for a long time and I travel constantly, so both brands are important to me. They both won my loyalty, and that of many others, of course, through these no-questions-asked guarantees. Bottom line: I trust these guarantees, so I invest in these products.

OPEN PHILANTHROPY

Being open and forthright is even more important when your business has a philanthropic component—being clear about where your donors' money will go is the best way to build their trust. A good case in point is the company called charity: water, run by Scott Harrison, who has taught me much about how to run an organization.

Scott's story inspires me as well. At the age of thirty-five he has already lived through many intense moments. The first took place when he was four years old: A carbon monoxide leak in his home resulted in his mother becoming an invalid for life, her immune system irreparably destroyed. Scott spent much of his childhood taking care of her.

In fact, he grew up, he says, "the perfect child." His conservative Christian parents taught him a rigid set of family values that he followed at home and in church. He lived those principles daily, taking care of his mother, cleaning, cooking, and going to services regularly.

But at eighteen years old, "I rebelled against everything." He grew his hair long, joined a rock band, and moved to New York City, hoping to become rich and famous. The rock band broke up four months later, but Scott became involved in the nightclub business and for the next ten years was one of the city's most successful nightclub promoters and party planners.

Still, at twenty-eight, Scott felt he was spiraling downward into a life of unbridled decadence. Then one day in 2004, while lying on the perfect beach in Uruguay with the perfect girlfriend, drinking the perfect cocktail, he realized how far he had drifted from the core values his parents had taught him. Deciding to return to theology to explore his faith and his life, he made a promise to God to serve the poor and began looking for volunteer opportunities in Africa.

Scott applied to several humanitarian organizations; the only one that accepted him was Mercy Ships, a charity offering help to people in need in ports around the world. He went as a photojournalist. Soon he set sail for Liberia, an impoverished country just coming out of civil war.

Two years later Scott was $40,000 in debt: "But my life had forever changed. I decided to dedicate the rest of my life in service to God and to the poor. Still, the more I discovered, the more I despaired."

When Scott learned that 80 percent of all disease on the planet was related to a lack of clean water and basic sanitation, and that 1.1 billion people did not have access to this most basic need, he decided to start a charity himself.

Most people Scott knew were suspicious of charities. They didn't trust the lack of transparency—but Scott thought he could fix that with a different model. *Be bold*, he thought. *Be direct, be simple, be open.* As clear as the clean water he wanted to make available to those in need. In fact, he named his charity for water.

He then implemented the "100 percent model." Every dollar charity: water took in from the public was to go directly to the field, to water projects. It would prove that all its work was real. Charity: water trained its field partners to use GPS devices and cameras so all of their projects could be put up on the Internet, allowing everyone who gave money to see exactly what that money was buying. The idea was to create a brand that everyone could trust—and one that looked good.

Five years later, charity: water has raised $22 million from more than 100,000 donors around the world. It has given one million people access to clean water in seventeen countries. "We have solved about .01 percent of the global water problem. Our ten-year goal is to help one hundred million people get access to clean water by 2020.

"It's all about trust. People know that when they give us money it will be used to do exactly what we say it will be used to do."

Charity: water has administrative costs, with twenty-six employees in New York and Scott's constant travel around the globe. But those costs are raised and allocated differently from the charity itself, so people who contribute to charity: water always know where their money is going.

I first met Scott in 2007 when we were both in the early stages of getting our organizations going. He spoke with a deep conviction about giving people clean water, and he did it with an entrepreneurial optimism I hadn't heard be-

Our Korean distributor, Deejay Lim, hugging kids in South Africa. Because of Deejay's incredible work, South Korea is one of TOMS' biggest international markets.

fore. Scott has greatly inspired me to do whatever it takes to make TOMS a success, and he taught me important lessons about building trust throughout our organizations—and with those who join our cause.

One of the ways we have done that is by taking our customers with us on our Shoe Drops, special trips to visit our giving partners and learn more about their work. When TOMS was younger, we accepted online applications—thousands of people of all ages and backgrounds applied; among those who were chosen to go with us were eighty-year-old grandmothers and eighteen-year-old college students. All in all, we have taken fifty trips, bringing along around 200 people.

By taking customers and other interested parties with us and encouraging them to post pictures and videos of their experience online, we develop trust beyond that group—it extends to customers who don't get to go on a drop but stumble on a video or picture online. They see us doing exactly the work TOMS promises to do.

We've also made it clear to our customers from the very beginning that our company is not like most others in the social-impact sector—we are a *for-profit* company. Our goal is to help people and to make money doing it. We have never hidden that from anyone and in so doing have paved the way for a new type of social venture.

TIPS FOR TRUST

As should be obvious by now, building trust is not only a business strategy or even just a nice thing to do. It is mission critical. Whether you're starting a corporation, a social enterprise, a nonprofit, or are working within an existing organization where you have a degree of autonomy, begin your new venture by stating your goals clearly and regularly. The more you articulate where you are going and what you are doing, the more your employees, customers, and funders will feel they can be a part of your goals, ensuring that they will trust the company's vision.

L et's review some tips that will help you win trust with all of these groups.

To foster trust within your organization:

TALK OPENLY WITH YOUR STAFF

For example, compliment publicly and criticize privately, but do both directly. If an employee makes a mistake, say so. Don't tell other people, or pretend it didn't happen, or cover up for him or her. People are putting their livelihoods in your hands as a leader. When you offer honest, constructive criticism, they'll feel more comfortable putting that trust in you.

Also, show some emotion when talking to your people. No need to be a cold fish. Revealing your true self makes you more real to everyone around you. And the more real you are, the more they'll trust you. Of course, you can show your joy and your pleasure too, but, when appropriate, openly show your weakness, frustration, and pain.

GIVE AWAY AUTONOMY

As more and more leaders work remotely or with teams scattered around the nation or the globe, as well as with consultants and freelancers, you'll have to give them more autonomy. The more trust you bestow, the more others trust you. I am convinced that there is a direct correlation between job satisfaction and how empowered people are to fully execute their job without someone shadowing them every step of the way.

Giving away responsibility to those you trust can not only make your organization run more smoothly but also free up more of your time so you can focus on larger issues. This means avoiding micromanagement. Involve yourself actively only at the beginning and end of a project, giving others the freedom and creativity to guide it along the way. When you micromanage, you're effectively telling people that you don't trust their judgment and that, unless you're personally involved in every detail, the project won't get done right. That attitude hardly inspires confidence.

TRUST THAT YOUR EMPLOYEES WILL GROW INTO THEIR ROLES

A perfect example of following this advice involves Jonathan, our first intern, who came to us straight out of graduate school with zero experience in handling logistics or

TRUST INTERNS

Interns are people too. Trust them. If you hire the right interns, you can treat them as responsible employees rather than coffee runners. At most companies, interns spend their time fetching coffee and making photocopies. At TOMS, interns work on the front lines and have real job responsibilities. When you put faith in people, you're often rewarded with a work ethic and passion that will blow away your expectations.

production—but it was clear that he was smart and trustworthy and that he would excel at whatever task we assigned him. Today, Jonathan has a senior role in TOMS' logistics, making sure that thousands of shoes get where they need to go every day, and he does a great job.

Sometimes when I talk about our employees, people respond that TOMS can get away with this kind of trust because we have such great people, while they don't. But that goes back to the issue of focusing your time on hiring the right staff. Spending extra time to find good people allows for more trust once you hire them, which frees up tremendous time (and anxiety) down the road. In their early days, many companies focus on getting people to fill up all the positions they've created and then spend too much time trying to manage them. If hiring excellent people becomes one of your top priorities, and the whole company pitches in together to make it a great process, you will wind up with excellent employees and a more trusting environment.

T o gain trust outside your organization:

ALWAYS FOLLOW THE GOLDEN RULE

The heart of great proactive customer service is empathy. If you ever enter into a dispute with a customer, treat him or her as you would like to be treated. And when customers have special needs, make them feel as special as you would want to feel.

For instance, not long ago, a woman called the TOMS general customer-service line asking if she could purchase two different-sized shoes as a pair (one in size 6, another in size 9.5). She was told that we don't make custom pairs and that she would have to order two pairs of shoes if she wanted to purchase two different-sized shoes. Two days later we received a long email from the woman, describing a medical condition known as clubfoot which had left her with different-sized feet. She explained that she'd had a tough time because other shoe companies had quoted her similar policies. Although she understood the issue, this was a special case: The TOMS wrap boot had just been introduced and she had to have a pair. She explained that the shoes she normally purchased were around fifty dollars a pair, meaning she could afford to buy two pairs if necessary, but at ninety-eight dollars the wrap boots were too expensive.

That's all we needed to hear. We contacted the warehouse, had them put together a custom pair of wrap boots, and even threw in a pair of custom-paired classics to make sure she had TOMS for all occasions. She was, she wrote back, thrilled—and so were we. We'd done the right thing and, in the process, we'd turned a simple customer into a potential evangelist for the brand.

To further trust if you're the founder of a nonprofit, follow the lead of Scott Harrison and charity: water.

BE AS OPEN AS POSSIBLE

Once again, openness is important no matter what your business or venture. The charity: water website includes a Google Map with location coordinates and photographs of every well it has built. When you look at the site, you see that there's no question that charity: water is doing what it says it's doing.

Many people are hesitant to give to nonprofits, because they don't know where or how their money is actually going to be used. This is why it can be a good idea to get individuals or an organization to underwrite your operational costs. This way, all the donations you collect go straight to the people you're working to help—making your donors feel confident their dollars are doing good things—and that only creates more generosity on their part.

Being open also encourages you to be frugal and responsible with the money you take in. If people are aware of where their money goes, you'll be less likely to spend it on a fancy office or high salaries.

USE YOUR OWN PRODUCTS

Finally, here's one more way to foster trust in your own organization. You can't truly tout your product or service to others unless you have a good sense of it yourself. Trust springs from knowledge. At TOMS, we work to fulfill this dictum however we can.

For example, when we launched TOMS wedges in the summer of 2010, after making a speech I was chatting with a woman who asked me if the wedges were comfortable. I said, "Yes." She then replied, "Well, how do you know that?"

The truth was that I didn't actually know, because I had never worn a pair of three-inch wedges before. The next time I was in the office, I did exactly that, much to the amusement of the TOMS staff. I wore them for two days straight; and I found out that the wedges really are comfortable—though pretty high for someone not accustomed to wearing heels.

seven

giving is good business

The more you give, the more you live.

—BOB DEDMAN

hile still in college, Lauren Bush enjoyed a career as a model and a volunteer. She was selected as an honorary spokesperson for the United Nations World Food Programme (WFP), a post that sent her to countries such as Guatemala, Cambodia, Sri Lanka, and Tanzania to see firsthand the effects of malnutrition and hunger on the world.

But the more countries she visited, the more disempowered she felt. "I came back from these trips wanting to help, but I didn't know what to do. Of course you want to lend a hand—but what can one person accomplish?"

Lauren began to study the issues surrounding global hunger, eventually realizing that giving kids something as simple as a free lunch could change their lives—and that it costs comparatively little to feed a child in school for a year: The world average ranges from twenty to fifty dollars.

At the same time that Lauren was traveling, she was also noticing that the reusable-bag movement was taking off. Providing a relatively easy way to become eco-friendly while shopping, reusable bags meant less strain on the environment. Lauren began looking into that too.

Then, in 2004, when she was twenty, Lauren had her epiphany: She could join the two ideas together by designing a fashion item that stood for more than fashion—namely, she would create a non-gender-specific, eco-friendly bag that would guarantee a child in a developing country a free year of school lunches for every bag sold.

The idea developed slowly, and by 2007, Lauren and her friend Elle Gustafson, who was working at the WFP at the time, partnered to create FEED Projects, which is what they call their "charitable company." They started to sell their bags exclusively on Amazon.com. As promised, for every one sold, a child received a year of school lunches. This was an idea I absolutely loved the first time I heard of it—a new variation of the TOMS model!

Lauren then started to reinvent the original bag, tagging each with different numbers to signify different giving levels: The FEED 2 bag feeds two children for one year, for example, and the FEED 100 bag provides one hundred school meals to a child in need in Rwanda. The company later diversified its philanthropy, giving to nutrition programs through UNICEF, to local literacy programs like Room to Read, and to FEED USA, a platform they created to support providing healthier school meals to kids in America as well. They've also created a "health backpack" to support community health workers in Millennium Villages in Africa.

To date, the company has sold more than 500,000 bags and donated enough money to provide more than 60 million school lunches around the world through the World Food Programme.

Nevertheless, FEED Projects is a for-profit company. Lauren is proud that the company makes enough money to sustain its ongoing operation while also providing her with a viable, profitable business that isn't dependent on charity. "Even though the project is all about feeding kids, we're able to do more than that. By giving kids a lunch meal in school, we're supporting their education also. For many kids, this is the only meal they'll get each day. So often we see kids take a portion of their lunch and put it in their pocket to bring it home for dinner, or perhaps to give it to another sibling not yet ready for school.

"I remember once, in Rwanda, asking a little girl what she wanted to be when she grew up. Sometimes you're afraid to ask this question, because the answer can be sad. But in this case, the little girl, who was now attending school and eating well, was confident and happy. 'I want to be president of Rwanda,' she said."

When Lauren told me this story, I melted. If a single FEED bag can help a child dream this big, then Lauren's company must be doing something right. And Lauren loves her work more than just about anyone I know. "Every day I wake up feeling lucky to be able to do this," she says.

GOOD^2

As FEED Projects demonstrates, giving is good business—in both senses of the word "good." It's good because it helps people; it's good because it makes money. It's a way to address two essential needs with an action that unifies them both. More and more people are finding this out and are creating businesses that make giving an essential component of their model.

I originally started TOMS as a spontaneous response to help those kids in Argentina obtain shoes in a sustainable way—and when the company started to work, when I went on that first Shoe Drop to give away the shoes, it was a life-changing experience. Giving felt good. But over the last few years, I've also experienced how giving is truly good for business as well.

If you incorporate giving into your business and life, you will see greater returns and rewards than you ever imagined. So many good things happen to you when giving is integrated into your business—and I'm not even talking about the wonderful results of the giving itself: the people across the world whose lives are improved because you have helped them. I'm talking about the business.

For one, when giving is incorporated into your model, your customers become your partners in marketing your product. Remember that story about the woman at the air-port who sold me on the TOMS story? TOMS has hun-dreds of similar anecdotes. For example, a young woman at Ohio State University loves TOMS so much that she or-ganized a large SYS (Style Your Soul) event in the fall of 2009—all on her own, reaching out to local high schools to educate them about TOMS and busing in high school stu-dents to be part of OSU's One Day Without Shoes barefoot walk.

Or, at University High School in Orlando, Florida, a teenager set up an assembly to show our documentary and asked the administration to help him share the TOMS movement. As a result of his efforts, the school volleyball team took a lap barefoot around the gym to raise awareness, and now the other teams go barefoot before their games to spread the TOMS message.

And at Ravenwood High School in Brentwood, Ten-nessee, several young students created "Operation TOMS Prom," getting more than 3,200 students from high schools across the country to wear TOMS to their prom.

Here is what the Ravenwood boys wrote about their experience: "A few of us here at Ravenwood High have been pretty passionate about what TOMS is doing for a while now, and with the up-and-coming prom season—a time usually marked by drama and expensive shopping sprees—we thought it would be really awesome if it turned into something bigger than ourselves. Something with which we could give instead of receive. Not many students in our area knew about TOMS and their mission, but those of us already involved decided to make the 'One for One' project school-wide while utilizing the prom as a catalyst to promote the cause and give what we thought would be a few hundred kids shoes. The idea has taken off quicker than any of us expected, not only in our school, but in schools spanning from the East Coast to the Midwest, with 35 participating schools already confirmed."

TOMS for PROM is now a nationwide campaign, giving tens of thousands of kids a new pair of desperately needed shoes each year.

SEAN THE SHOE DOG

Sean was one of the first people to join me on this journey. He is a Shoe Dog, someone who works in the shoe business. Before that, he was a dedicated triathlete, and the only jobs that would support his athletic habit were those in athletic-goods stores, so that's where he worked, part-time.

He eventually started to work full-time with Nike; in fact, Sean held several jobs in the corporate footwear world before he and a friend created a skate-shoe company: 2•fish shoe works. However, that company eventually folded, and Sean decided to become an independent shoe consultant.

Sean and I met for the first time in 2006, just after the *Los Angeles Times*

article about TOMS had come out and we needed help, fast.

Here's what Sean has to say:

I met with Blake, liked him, and thought, OK, here's a job just like the others. The One for One idea seemed cute. I didn't have a clue if it was viable, but Blake convinced me to help him. That was in July of 2006. In October, TOMS had sold 10,000 pairs of shoes and was planning its first Shoe Drop. This also happened to be my ninth wedding anniversary, so I thought a trip would make a great anniversary present.

By the end of the Shoe Drop, I knew it wasn't just a nice present. It was a life-changing event. At the first stop, a wonderful woman who ran an orphanage told me that more than

If you are doing good, customers have a greater reason to care about your work. That is why Pepsi made a surprise move at the 2010 Super Bowl. Normally, Pepsi and Coke compete to show the best commercials on the air, spending a great deal of money to do so. But Pepsi opted out of advertising and instead took the $20 million it would have spent and set up the Pepsi Refresh Project online, giving the money away to people who could come up with the best idea for a better tomorrow.

anything else, shoes were what she needed; otherwise, the kids couldn't get an education. I cried. In fact, I must have burst into tears at least three times on that trip.

This caught both me and my wife, Shannon, off guard. We were changing the lives of many people. This is why Blake tries to get so many employees to go on the Shoe Drops. No one comes back the same. And that's what makes working at TOMS different. No matter how tough the day, or no matter how difficult a customer, you get to pick your head up, take a deep breath, and say, "I don't care, I am making a difference. I went there. I put shoes on their feet. I saw the tears on their faces. I saw the smiles on their mothers' faces. I made a difference."

My wife and I decided that we had to get our two kids to see this, too,

to understand that materialism isn't everything and that big houses and big cars aren't all that matters. So in January of 2008 the whole Scott family went down to Argentina on another Shoe Drop. My kids were not just impressed—I can honestly say they are proud of me. They want to wear my shoes. That's never been the case before. It makes me feel good.

The rewards of giving are enormous—not just for the recipients, but for you too. It helps you get through a bad day. You love talking about your job. You love your job. When I first came to TOMS, I was jaded. I had met too many business leaders who created an inspiring message but didn't practice it. I thought I'd never be inspired again by my career. Now I am.

As part of our collaboration with Element, we made a limited-edition line of shoes and One for One skateboards. This picture was taken at the Indigo Skate Camp outside Durban.

For Pepsi, not only does the campaign help nourish hundreds of ideas that could become the next big business or philanthropic movement, but it also establishes Pepsi as an intrinsic part of that new company's formation and history, creating a strong bond between it and the new company's customers.

And it goes beyond creating loyal customers; you also attract and retain the most amazing employees when you incorporate giving into your business. People often tell us that TOMS has remarkable people working for us—and we do. We are able to find terrific people who want to be a part of the TOMS story. And our employees stay. Over the years, TOMS has lost only a handful, and at the same time we have been able to get extraordinary people to step away from corporate America and forgo the typical perks of working for Fortune 500 companies. Instead, they've come on board to make a difference with us.

According to a new survey on corporate community involvement released by auditing and consulting firm Deloitte, 72 percent of employed Americans say they would prefer to work for a company that supports charitable causes when they are deciding between two jobs with the same location, responsibilities, pay, and benefits. Similarly, in its own 2002 study, the communications agency Cone found that 77 percent of respondents said that a company's commitment to social issues was a major factor when deciding where to work.

Over and over I have seen that when people feel they are all working together to help others, office morale is high, and negative office politics don't tend to develop. This creates wonderful working conditions and helps attract and retain loyal employees.

THE HALO

Giving doesn't just make it easy to attract great employees; it also means you can attract great partners as well. After all, it's hard to start any business alone; you will always benefit from finding other people to lend you their name, their expertise, and even their company's resources. You'll quickly find that businesses want to partner with other businesses that are doing something good—and they root for you to succeed, because they admire your giving goals.

From our very first year, TOMS has been able to attract many different partners. We worked with Microsoft and AOL on One Day Without Shoes (ODWS), Threadless also participated by designing an ODWS T-shirt contest; Facebook, on our holiday campaigns; YouTube, in getting our story out there; and *Teen Vogue*, which created a Style Your Sole contest—just to name a few of the many organizations that have worked with us. A few others: Ralph Lauren, Digg's Kevin Rose, charity: water's Scott Harrison, and Element skateboards' Johnny Schillereff.

Moreover, very large companies seldom have giving programs that resonate with the public—too often, they look like tax write-offs or publicity gimmicks. But by partnering with smaller companies or nonprofits that are more hands-on, these large companies are able to help people better understand their brand's giving efforts while also raising employee morale.

They need us as much as we need them, and that's what makes these partnerships so great. For example, Saks Fifth Avenue gave charity: water every window on Fifth Avenue and raised $300,000 by selling charity: water bracelets and T-shirts. This was great for charity: water but also helped Saks' image and created much enthusiasm among Saks employees.

Similarly, Gap partnered with Lauren Bush's FEED to make three shoulder bags; five dollars from each sale went directly to FEED. The bag also came with a DonorsChoose code so that the money would be given to a school of the buyer's choice.

Another example: *GOOD* magazine, "the integrated

media platform for people who want to live well and do good," partnered with Starbucks to create the GOOD Sheet, an info-graphic that highlighted such hot-button issues as education, healthcare, and carbon emissions.

And another: Frito-Lay North America (a division of PepsiCo) formed a partnership with TerraCycle to take used Frito-Lay packages and turn them into quality goods. The program encourages consumers and local community groups to earn money by collecting the used packaging and at the same time redirect packaging from landfills. This program feeds right into TerraCycle's purpose and also allows Frito-Lay to get more out of their giving.

Just as TOMS outsources technology because we are not a technology company, these large companies partner with cause-related organizations because it's not their core competency. Both companies benefit from the arrangement— and, more important, it exponentially increases the amount of good that gets accomplished.

This is even true for TOMS. While our roots are in Shoe Drops, our global shoe giving is now accomplished through humanitarian organizations with deep roots in the communities in which they operate. They serve children in a holistic way, through health, education, clean water, and more. And they integrate our shoes into their programs for even greater impact. Their ongoing presence means we can get shoes to kids again and again as they grow. Shoe Drops are still a means for us to visit these organizations and help place shoes on kids' feet, but these partnerships have made our global giving possible, as well as more powerful.

THE NEW BUSINESS MODEL

Despite the fact that making giving an essential part of business is a win-win, it hasn't always been in favor. In the past, many prominent economists and gurus have spoken out *against* corporate giving. The influential American economist Milton Friedman is often quoted as saying that the only social responsibility of business is to increase its profits. Period.

That was the reigning philosophy in mid-twentieth-century America, but such thinking is out of date and out of gas. Social and economic priorities are merging. Companies realize that a profits-only focus risks alienating customers and partners. They also know that if they want to attract the best talent, they have to pay attention to having a positive social impact; remember the 2006 Cone study showing that 80 percent of respondents said they wanted to work for a company that cares about its impact on society. Likewise, a 2008 study from Stanford University business school found that 97 percent of the students polled would forgo financial benefits to work for a company that had a better reputation for corporate social responsibility.

Most large corporations, from Prudential to IBM, from 3M to Sears, have programs that give back to the community, many for obvious reasons: Apple donates hundreds of computers to schools, which helps education as well as creating a market for Apple products. American Express funds Travel and Tourism Academies in secondary schools—the more people there are trained to help those who travel, the more people will travel using American Express cards. Home-improvement retailer Home Depot has partnered with the child-oriented nonprofit KaBOOM! to build 1,000 playgrounds in 1,000 days, putting $25 million into the initiative and getting almost 100,000 Home Depot employees to volunteer in some way. Kroger supermarkets give local nonprofits cards that allow users to buy groceries at 5 percent off the retail price. The nonprofits then sell these cards and retain the difference.

Other companies have created programs that are less obviously connected to their brand but are instead based on a sense of doing what is right—and that helps to create a strong sense of customer loyalty. For example, shoe company Timberland allows full-time employees to take a week off from the office to work with its own service initiative called Path of Service. Each employee can pick whichever project he or she wishes and is paid a regular weekly salary. As a result, Timberland has a very high employee retention rate.

THE GIVING INITIATIVE

As you can see, I highly recommend that anyone starting a business incorporate giving into its essence. But you don't have to be starting something to make a difference. Sometimes, in fact, having an impact can spring from the efforts of wonderful people taking the initiative within an existing company. For example, here's a story from bestselling author and consultant Tim Sanders about some thoughtful employees at the Canadian bank CIBC, which he described in his manifesto on corporate responsibility, *Saving the World at Work.*

In 1997, the community-relations group of CIBC's Edmonton, Alberta, branch signed on to sponsor the Canadian Breast Cancer Foundation's annual Run for the Cure fund-raiser. The sponsorship program offered a modest amount of financial support and encouraged CIBC employees to participate, by either running in the event or pledging money to those who did.

For the next three years, hundreds of tellers from Edmonton to Toronto decided that they wanted to give as much as they could; they signed up to run for the fund-raiser, organized teams at each of the branch locations to strategize how to raise more money, and participated in corporate promotions, putting up posters and wearing T-shirts and pink ribbons provided by the Canadian Breast Cancer Foundation.

By 2001, after thousands of CIBC employees had joined in, senior bank executives asked the brand-marketing group to research the impact of the company's sponsorship. The resulting data suggested that it was driving the bank's popularity with customers, especially women, and that a side benefit was a boost in employee retention.

Because of these efforts and their results, bank executives then reclassified the program as strategic to the company, moving it from their community-affairs department to the powerful and well-funded brand-marketing group. They also approved an additional three million dollars in sponsorship money to promote the event through television, print, and Web advertisements. Today, Race for the Cure is the largest breast cancer fund-raising event in North America—all because CIBC employees got together to make sure that their company gave back to its community. In 2010 they raised a record $33 million.

Even if you're not going to start a company that matters, you can still start something small that can be built into something that matters in a very big way.

Whoever you are and whatever you do, giving is important. Start now. Start by helping other people—anyone you can. Do something simple. You don't have to start a business or big initiative right away—you can begin just by changing your mindset. Commit to seeing the world through the lens of how you can initiate meaningful change.

I founded my first company when I was nineteen years old, but none of my early companies, or even my free time, had anything to do with charity or giving. That wasn't part of my worldview then.

But when I began to realize what I should—and what I could—do, everything changed. I made a life choice and switched to this mode of interaction with the world. It was a very difficult decision to make when starting something new; I could have waited until the business was mature and then created some tax write-offs. But it was an important decision to move forward early, because if you wait a long time before you act, you won't gain all of the benefits mentioned in this chapter. Needless to say, I'm glad I made that decision.

GIVING FROM THE CORE

Don't make giving an afterthought. If it resonates with you, figure out how to responsibly make it a part of what you are creating. Here are some more tips to help you incorporate giving into your organization:

GIVE MORE THAN MONEY

Money is wonderful, and necessary, but there are plenty of other ways to become involved besides making financial donations. And while I would never downplay the importance of money, remember that the more you're actively involved in your giving, the more fulfilling it will be for you, and the more it will become a part of your everyday life. When you give only money, you often don't know where it goes, and you seldom see its results.

THINK ABOUT YOUR SPECIAL SKILLS

Everyone has some talent that they can donate to others. If you're a dentist, offer to do pro bono teeth cleanings for families that couldn't otherwise afford your services. If you're a writer, offer to write up publicity and promotion pieces for a nonprofit that needs help. Scott Harrison has an accountant who has raised many hundreds of thousands of dollars for charity: water because he works with many

The Official TOMS Couple, Sara and Jordan Maslyn, share a smooch on their wedding day.

wealthy clients; as their accountant, he knows exactly how much they can afford to write off at the end of the year!

INCORPORATE GIVING
ANYWHERE YOU CAN AT WORK

Let others know about your giving as often as you can, whether it's through marketing campaigns, vacations, relationships, dates, etc. Soon you will find yourself surrounded

THOUGHTFUL GIVING

Giving is a wonderful act—but giving responsibly is essential to having true impact. Here are some tips on thoughtful giving from two people who know a great deal about the subject: Candice Wolfswinkel, TOMS' Chief Giving Officer, and Jessica Shortall, TOMS' Director of Giving.

1. Always listen to the people and organizations you wish to help. In other words, don't give based on your needs. Give based on the needs of the organization and people you wish to serve. Design your product, offer your service, donate your money, or volunteer your time based on what the organization you wish to help

needs, not on what you want to give. Commit to always listening and always learning.

2. Don't create a situation in which your gift contains hidden costs to the recipient. Ask questions about the entire cost of delivering your gift and, if you can, cover as many of these costs as possible.

    For example, if you were to give someone, say, shoes, perhaps all they'd end up with is a big pile of shoes—organizations have to pay for transportation (trucks, cars, and even donkeys!), temporary storage, meals for volunteers who are helping out, and so on. If you're giving your time as a volunteer, figure out with like-minded people. For instance, TOMS received this great story on Valentine's Day of a couple whose marriage was inspired by TOMS.

> *When we were in Virginia on vacation this past summer (from our home in CA), our delightful 22-year-old bearded, tattooed Web-designer son and our family were eating burgers at a little retro diner in Williamsburg. We were approached by a (brave!) girl. "My friend wanted me to give you her number" is what she told our son.*

your host organization's financial obligations; this could mean housing, transportation, food, or time.

3. Put as few restrictions as possible on your gift (within the constraints of giving responsibly of course!). If you trust the organization, trust that they will use your resources in the most effective way possible.

4. When you give, keep your requirements for reporting simple and straightforward. At TOMS, we'd never ask one of our giving partners to send us a photo and the name of every child who receives shoes—they have too much work to do to spend all day taking photos! Understand that what you are giving is one part of a complex set of services that most nonprofit organizations are delivering. Ask your giving partners what information other donors are requiring for reporting to try to save them time on formatting and presentation, while still making sure you receive the critical information you need to complete your own mission.

5. Keep seeking feedback to improve your giving. Poverty, health initiatives, climate change, disaster relief: No cause is easy to solve, and no one will get it perfect on the first try. Ask for feedback on how your gift of time, money, or resources is or is not working, and then go back to point #1. Listen and don't be afraid to make changes.

Yes, this cute and stylish 20-year-old thought our son was cute . . . but what clinched it was that he was wearing TOMS! Because he was fashionable AND socially conscious, she could NOT let this opportunity pass by! He called her. They dated cross-country (interrupted briefly by his six-week trip to help orphans in Kenya). They are now planning their Virginia wedding and they want everyone in the wedding party (bride, groom, attendants, flower girls—parents???) to wear TOMS!

The story went right up on our blog!

GIVE EARLY

Start giving now, so you can enjoy the benefits throughout your life. In the old model, you waited until you turned sixty-five and retired before thinking about giving. There's no need to wait anymore. Give until you're sixty-five, and then give some more. If you find ways to make giving core to your business—or to your recreation or profession or even your existing job—you don't have to deliver a lump sum to your favorite charity at some hazy point in the future: You can give every day of your life in the increments that make the most sense to you.

DON'T GET OVERWHELMED

If you look at all the terrible troubles the world faces, you may feel helpless to do anything. So simplify things and just think about one issue, even one person. For example, a microloan website like Kiva.org allows you to help banks make loans to individuals for a specific project, such as to someone in Uganda who needs a goat for a small business. You can help that enterprise to sustain itself—and someday you'll also get your money back. Changing just one person's life can be a wonderful blessing.

IT'S BETTER TO GIVE THAN TO RECEIVE

Create selfless ways for people to help. For instance, Scott Harrison created a Birthday Campaign, in which participants forgo presents and a party by asking friends to donate their age in money to charity: water. This campaign has been enormously successful, and some people with a great many friends—such as marketing guru Seth Godin—have been able to raise as much as $50,000 in one day (not because he's that old, but because he has that many friends).

LISTEN TO THOSE YOU GIVE TO

No matter what you are giving—money, time, or even shoes—the people and organizations working on the front lines probably know more about how to use those resources effectively. Ask questions, truly listen, and then tailor your gift so that it is even more impactful.

eight

the final step

The best way to find yourself is to lose yourself in the service of others.

—Mahatma Gandhi

I would like to share with you a letter I recently received from a young man named Tyler Eltringham, the founder of OneShot, a wonderful organization that helps people receive meningitis vaccinations, both in America and in Africa.

Dear Blake,

A few months prior to starting my freshman year in college at Arizona State University, I discovered

TOMS Shoes. A close friend of mine had shown me her pair of TOMS and then explained the concept of One for One. The shoes could have been the most hideous pieces of apparel on the planet and I still would have purchased multiple pairs, knowing how it was helping an individual elsewhere. But I really liked them!

My first pair were black canvas, and for the first two months I owned them I must have worn them every single day, because my friends told me it seemed like the shoes had become my second skin. The next semester, I purchased another pair as a "Congratulations, you made it through another semester of school!" present to myself; this became somewhat of a tradition, and now every semester I buy another pair.

A little background: I'm not the traditional college student. When I was five years old my parents got divorced; my mom and I packed our bags and moved from Pennsylvania to Arizona to start a brand-new life. Growing up, I always pushed myself into leadership roles, whether that meant barking out orders to stuffed animals on my playground as I led them into a fierce war, or soaking up the opportunities that Student Council had to offer.

Flash-forward to high school: My mom, who is also my best friend, fell very ill with pancreatitis and grand mal epilepsy. My stepdad had to quit his job to take care of her full-time, and our financial situation darkened. For three years we battled poverty and on-and-off homelessness, but the entire time my mom never gave up hope for my future. For instance, she once went without her pain medication for weeks to save up enough money to ensure I had a good Christmas. That image of selflessness still buckles my knees.

When her condition worsened, I dropped out of high school and got my GED, hoping to advance my life faster so I could be a provider for them, as they were for me. Seeing her passed from doctor to doctor with no one wanting to take ownership of her disease infuriated me. It became the catalyst for my next move.

Through a few acts of serendipity, I enrolled at Arizona State University as a Barack Obama Scholar. There, wanting a truly interdisciplinary education, I entered the Bachelor of Science program in Geographical Sciences and embedded myself into my community, meeting many incredible people and becoming involved in some wonderful organizations (the President of the Geography Honor Society, a Pat Tillman Scholar, and ASU's community of entrepreneurship and innovation).

One day, after reading about the ASU Innovation Challenge, a college competition for people hoping to get seed funding for big ideas, I sat there thinking for a few moments before switching positions and crossing my legs. I looked down at my shoes, which happened to be TOMS, and started thinking "One for One . . . so much could be accomplished with that sort of movement. Is it possible to incorporate my passion for health and medicine with the One for One movement?"

I can't say exactly what happened next, but I had an idea, based on a disease I'd heard about when I was preparing to move into my residence hall my freshman year: meningococcal meningitis.

A little background: Meningococcal meningitis is a bacterial infection that claims the lives of nearly 2,600 people in the U.S. every year—although it is most common in Africa, where more than 75,000 suspected cases were reported in fourteen neighboring countries that make up Africa's "meningitis belt," the earth's largest confluence of meningitis.

The infection causes inflammation of the membrane surrounding a human's brain and spinal cord, leading to symptoms such as fever, stiff neck, and headache. Without immediate medical treatment, death can arrive in as few as two days, and even with early medical attention, up to 20 percent of patients will still die. Among the survivors of the infection's initial onslaught, more than 20 percent will experience permanent and life-changing ailments such as deafness, blindness, learning disabilities, or nervous system damage.

Meningococcal disease occurs all over the world, even in the U.S., 7,400 miles from the meningitis belt. Being a communicable disease and very easily transmitted in close quarters such as dormitories and other university housing options, meningococcal meningitis is not only one of *our* country's most silent and deadly predators, it is common on college campuses.

It is also *completely preventable* with vaccination.

The idea was simple: College students need vaccinations, and the populations within the meningitis belt of Africa needed vaccinations. If I could somehow convince my peers to get vaccinated, while vaccinating the meningitis belt in the process . . . it might just work!

This is OneShot: a nonprofit organization that provides meningococcal meningitis vaccinations to college students living in dormitories and university housing, while also addressing the global issue at hand. For every single vaccine administered stateside, OneShot donates a vaccine to the meningitis belt of Africa.

While studying marketing, I learned that consumers don't buy products. They buy solutions. So my idea was to create a *local* solution to a *global* challenge, applying TOMS' One for One initiative toward preventative medicine and epidemiology.

I had never self-identified as an entrepreneur; I was just determined to make a difference while moving my career forward. Heck, I was a pre-med student at the time! Starting OneShot was hardly a walk in the park. While we had amazing ideas and plenty of passion to drive us forward, it wasn't easy to gain the trust of people who mattered, people who needed to believe in a group of college kids who wanted to save the world. Only one of our organization's officers had a traditional business background, so formulating our business plan and proposals were challenges, as were crafting a story that was easy to believe in while proving that our idea was sustainable and economically feasible.

We didn't let this stop us. When we competed in the ASU Innovation Challenge, we pitched our brains out to a group of judges from around the country: experts in entrepreneurship and venture start-ups. With the help of my mentors Dr. Michael Mokwa and Dr. Denise Link at ASU, the backing of two amazing individuals in Steve Thompson and Gail Hock, and the support of a team of dedicated peers (who just happen to be my best friends)— Corey Frahm, Ginger Whitesell, Geoff Prall, Tyler Liss, and Amy Weihmuller—OneShot took home the $10,000 grand prize of the ASU Innovation Challenge!

Now we knew that if we were capable of convincing industry professionals that our idea was worth investing in, it was worth investing our own lives into it as well—and we did.

As OneShot became more recognized in the entrepreneurial sphere, opportunities came our way. Suddenly organizations approached us, wanting to help shape our business: We had the backing of our entire university, as well as our local vaccine and immunization partnerships and advocacy groups; and even groups like the U.S. Centers for Disease Control and Prevention were interested in our initiatives. Media and news outlets started contacting us for publicity, and soon we were on the cover of the *Phoenix Business Journal,* the *State Press,* and even on ABC News Radio and ABC College News!

As of today, OneShot is fighting the uphill battles of a traditional business start-up. My team of officers and I are all full-time students who also have jobs to pay the bills, but OneShot is a constant top priority. We are currently finalizing the logistics for our first big vaccine drive for our 2011 Fall Move-In, immunizing freshmen who are moving into their residence halls: We're expecting over 1,200 students! We're working with ASU, the College of Nursing and Health Innovation, and the Maricopa County Department of Public Health to ensure that the success of our event was worth all of the struggles we put forth to organize the initiative.

In a perfect world, OneShot will eventually be acquired by a larger company with more resources, and we can transform from a meningitis-shot company into a One for One vaccination company, covering a wide range of preventable diseases.

To be honest, it's all really frightening that, despite all our hard work, there's no way of knowing if it will work in the long run. I know everyone has these kinds of doubts. It's still scary. But no matter what happens, OneShot has taught our team so many lessons, the payout is unquantifiable. The experience has been truly life changing: I am no longer pre-med. My passion is in helping others on a much larger scale. I have become incredibly attached to seeing OneShot become successful, and leaving a legacy in which we aid communities that would otherwise not have been given help.

Thank you, Blake, for inspiring me to do what I can to save the world.

People often ask me what I consider to be my goal at TOMS. The truth is that it's changed over the years. When we first began, the goal was to create a for-profit company that could help relieve the pain and suffering felt by children around the world who do not have shoes. And that objective continues to be a powerful driver for me and everyone else at TOMS.

But recently my attitude has shifted. Today I would say that my goal is to influence other people to go out into the world and have a positive impact, to inspire others to start something that matters, whether it's a for-profit business or a nonprofit organization. I feel a deep sense of responsibility to share everything we have learned at TOMS, so that as many others as possible can start something important. That's why letters like Tyler's move me so much. In fact, I get more joy from hearing those kinds of stories than from almost anything else.

Tyler is only one of many out there who are taking that wonderful and courageous step forward, who are moving from thinking about doing something to actually doing it. People are always telling me that there's something they want to do or that they have a goal they want to accomplish but that they don't have the confidence to start or that their idea isn't a big one like TOMS.

I remind them that TOMS was just an idea in my journal when we started. As I wrote in Chapter 5, start with something simple. Don't worry about being large. Every big company you see today was once small.

None of the people mentioned in this book said they were so confident when they began that they knew they were starting a large business or a major nonprofit. They just felt compelled to start something. So they did.

Scott Harrison volunteered with Mercy Ships, and this experience led to his idea for charity: water. Lauren Bush became a spokesperson for the World Food Programme, and being a volunteer changed her life and the lives of kids all over the world as well because it moved her to create FEED.

You don't have to have a lot of money, a complicated business plan, or a great deal of experience to start something. Start small, and maybe you'll stay small, which is fine. Or maybe you'll get bigger. I never thought that TOMS would occupy my whole life. I started it as a side project while working on another company.

Remember the poem at the beginning of this book:

To know even one life has breathed easier
because you have lived—
This is to have succeeded.

You don't have to start something with a goal of saving the world. You don't have to create a Falling Whistles or invent a FEED bag. If whatever you do helps just one person, you've done something wonderful. If I receive a letter from someone who started something small and who helped two kids who might not otherwise have been helped—that means the world to me.

The most important step of all is the first step. Start something! What if that idea you have in the back of your head is a really good one, one that might end up helping tens of thousands of people? You owe it to the world to act. Or maybe it will help only a few people: The same advice applies. If you don't do it, you are missing out on something big, and so are the people who could have been helped.

Someone once told me the key to staying healthy was tying his shoes. What he meant was, once he actually put his shoes on and tied them, then he would go out for a run. And by going for a run, he was able to stay very healthy.

That same philosophy applies here. The first step to starting the journey is simply to put on your shoes—that's all. Then tie your shoelaces. Just because that first step is a very simple one doesn't mean that it can't lead someday to something profound.

Not only is taking that first step less difficult than you may imagine, but it may change your life in wonderful ways. Once you start helping others, you will notice this change—you will feel less sad, less stressed, and more purposeful. This isn't wishful thinking on my part. I have seen this happen over and over.

If it isn't clear already, I firmly believe that every person alive can make this world a better place. I also believe that we are all equipped to help one another. Just as we all have five senses, we all are born with the ability to improve another person's life. And that means everyone reading this book has the potential to make a difference. So in the next few moments, as you finish this book, I ask you to please put it down and think about whatever plans have been running through your mind. Let those ideas move from the back to the front of your mind. Take this time to write them down in your journal or call a friend or relative to discuss them. Get your idea out in the open. Decide that you can do this. Tell yourself you're not going to let this thought go unnoticed.

Then I want you to take the next step. Start something that matters.

For me, the ultimate success of this book will be measured not by how many copies it sells but by the number of people it inspires and the number of letters we receive. So please keep me posted by posting your story at www.startsome thingthatmatters.com.

I look forward to hearing from you.

Carpe diem,

Blake

acknowledgments

If I were to acknowledge everyone who helped me in the course of TOMS' history, this section might be as long as the book itself. Truly, TOMS' success is not the result of an idea, but a community of people who believe in the power of giving and who have supported the One for One model from the beginning. This community includes customers, giving partners, retailers, interns, campus clubs, international distributors, sales reps, retail advocates, board members, corporate partners, collaborators, editors, bands, PR firms, and personal mentors. The support of this community, and the tireless work of all the TOMS family (aka our employees), is the reason that millions of children have received much-needed shoes. It is because of you all that a simple idea has transformed into a company, and even greater than that, a movement. Thank you.

I also want to thank all of my friends who have put up with my constant absences, given all the crazy travel I've had to do the past few years. The fact that I can pop in after being gone for months and feel as if I never left is the sign of true friendship. Your love and support mean the world to me—as do the love and support of my parents, Mike and Pam, and my brother, Tyler, and my sister, Paige, who have been critical to my being able to believe that this crazy idea might actually work. From Paige helping me design the logo, to Tyler starting as an intern sleeping on my couch, having you both so intimately involved since the beginning has been a gift.

Thanks go to Alejo Nitti; the only polo instructor turned accountant turned shoemaker I'll ever meet, for always believing in my crazy ideas and being with me every step of the way. To Alejo's parents, Hilda Capello and Ricardo Nitti, Alejo's wife, Natalia, and the entire TOMS family in Argentina, for having patience with my Spanish and for always treating me as one of their own. None of this would have been possible without your generosity and love.

I also want to thank all the people at Random House who have done so much to help, especially Cindy Spiegel, Julie Grau, Avideh Bashirrad, and, especially, my excellent editor, Chris Jackson. I'd also like to thank Chip Gibson of Random House Children's Books and Melanie Fallon-Houska of Random House Corporate Giving for helping to facilitate the One for One initiative for the book. Likewise, thanks to my agent, David Vigliano, and to Adam Korn for taking me around to meet all the great publishers. I am also grateful to everyone who was interviewed for the book, especially those who "started something that matters" and who have inspired me so much. And, at TOMS, I want to express my gratitude to Jake Strom for all his research, creativity, and constant brainstorming, and to Candice Wolfs-winkel for her editing and eternal kindness.

Finally, a note about my co-writer, Gene Stone, who has been such an amazing writing partner, mentor, and friend for the past few years. Little did you know at that first breakfast meeting that you would play such an important role at TOMS. I am so grateful for everything you have done.

And last, but certainly not least, to the millions of TOMS fans around the world who have helped to spread the One for One movement. Together, and one pair of shoes at a time, I truly believe that we've started something that matters.

start something That Matters

BLAKE MYCOSKIE

A READER'S GUIDE

chapter one: the TOMS story

Blake Mycoskie, founder of TOMS, describes the idea that would come to define TOMS' business model: "With every pair you purchase, TOMS will give a pair of new shoes to a child in need. One for One."™ Key to TOMS' growth has been the company's commitment to giving. It attracts customers, inspires employees, generates media attention, and appeals to partners who also want to give back. Blake then identifies the six elements that have helped TOMS to flourish. These six principles—Find Your Story, Face Your Fears, Be Resourceful Without Resources, Keep It Simple, Build Trust, and Giving Is Good Business—serve as the focus of each of the following chapters.

DISCUSSION QUESTIONS

1. How does the TOMS story appeal to customers? Employees? Business partners? The media?

2. TOMS is unusual in that it's a for-profit company that actively incorporates giving into its business model. Can you think of other examples of giving-based businesses? How are these companies similar to and different from TOMS?

3. Why might a for-profit business like TOMS be able to succeed in its charitable goals more effectively than a nonprofit? In what ways do for-profit businesses enjoy greater freedoms than nonprofits?

4. What are other global problems that could be addressed by giving-based businesses? What barriers prevent these problems from being addressed by governments and nonprofit organizations?

5. Could a giving-based business like TOMS have succeeded ten, twenty, or fifty years ago? How has consumer culture changed to make the TOMS business model not only viable, but also profitable?

WORDS INTO ACTION

1. **Connecting needs with your brand.** Spend an afternoon walking or driving around your community. Identify five societal needs that are not being met, such as homelessness, litter, or problems with public transportation. Now identify five products or services that could be created to address these challenges.

2. **What's your *alpargata*?** Blake identified the *alpargata* as a foreign product with commercial potential in the United States. Try to identify some of your own personal possessions that, in the past, would not have been considered commercially viable. What changed to make these products marketable?

3. **What's the story?** Over the next day or so, think about every company that you come into contact with—as a customer, employee, or passerby—and ask yourself, What is the company's story? How do they communicate their message? Are they missing a storytelling opportunity?

chapter two: find your story

Straightforward ads—*Ford trucks are the toughest; Crest toothpaste makes teeth their whitest*—aren't as effective as they used to be. Even if it's a proven fact that a product is the superior, it might not resonate with customers and clients unless it's embedded in a story. An engaging, meaningful story, Blake observes, immediately clarifies your brand's identity. It also attracts customers: If they find the story compelling, they suddenly have a reason to turn a thoughtless decision between competing brands into one that impacts the world in a meaningful way. Plus, customers can become part of the story by simply buying your product, a situation that benefits both the company and the customer. TOMS was built upon the story of giving. Chapter Two poses the important, first question: *What's your story?*

DISCUSSION QUESTIONS

1. As you begin to find your personal story, answer the three questions that Blake poses in Chapter Two: If you didn't have to worry about money, what would you do with your time? What kind of work would you do? What causes would you serve?

2. Consumers are savvier than ever before, and are often keenly aware of being manipulated by advertising. How can you make sure that people are moved by your story and not manipulated by it?

3. The business model for TOMS Shoes is really simple: "With every pair you purchase, TOMS will give a pair of new shoes to a child in need. One for One."™ Could a company exist that gives a *different* product than they sell? Would this be confusing to customers?

4. The TOMS story flowed out of a significant, powerful experience in Blake's life—an experience that caused him to see the world in a different light. Have you had any experiences like this in your own life? Could any of these experiences serve as a basis for your story?

5. Think of a few day-to-day products that you use, like toothpaste, laundry detergent, or underwear. If you could speak directly to the companies that make these products, what advice would you give them? What would make these products more memorable?

WORDS INTO ACTION

1. **Communication breakdown.** Notice what brands and products you are most loyal to. How could these companies communicate their stories more effectively? Through advertising? Corporate partnerships? By including giving in their business models?

2. **Free advertising.** Over the next week, begin paying attention to times when your friends do what the "airport girl" did—when they voluntarily advertise a product or service that they love. What brands do your friends talk about? What's a recent purchase that you've made because of a friend's recommendation?

3. **What's in a name?** TOMS contains part of the word "tomorrow," which suggests optimism and hope, key components in the TOMS story. Can you think of other companies that include the spirit of their mission in their name?

chapter three: *face your fears*

Thomas Edison famously said, "Many of life's failures are people who did not realize how close they were to success when they gave up." Pam Mycoskie, Blake's mom, could very easily have been added to the ranks of discouraged strivers who gave up just as they were about to break through. But she faced her fear, pushed through, and wrote a bestselling book. Fear occurs in response to situations in which you are exposed, at risk, or uncertain. It heightens your senses, but it can also freeze you in your tracks, because it's more than an emotion—it's a physiological state, too. You cannot control this. You can only control your actions. Once you realize this, it becomes easier to act despite your fear—to take action even though you are afraid.

DISCUSSION QUESTIONS

1. When has fear prevented you from achieving a goal in school, business, or in your personal life? In what form did this fear come up? How did you react to it?

2. What's the worst mistake that you've ever made? What was the end result? Were the consequences as bad as you thought they might be?

3. If you had no fear at all, how would you live your life differently? Would you change jobs or start a new business? Dedicate yourself to a favorite passion? Finally ask that special someone out on a date?

4. What are some strategies for dealing with fear while you are experiencing it? In what way is fear a *good* thing?

5. How does Blake relate the concept of "living your story" to overcoming fear?

WORDS INTO ACTION

1. **Dodging bullets.** Think of something you recently accomplished at work or school that was difficult. Now list all of the things that could have gone wrong, but didn't, that would have prevented you from reaching your goal. How did you avoid these pitfalls?

2. **Déjà vu all over again?** Sometimes fear is based upon experience: You encounter a situation that you've dealt with before where things went wrong, and you don't want to repeat the past. Sometimes it's irrational and isn't based upon anything at all. The next time you experience fear, analyze it. Is it a rational or an irrational fear?

3. **The only thing we have to fear . . .** Over the next day or so, try to count every business that you come into contact with.

Then reflect on the fact that every one of those businesses—from the mom-and-pop store to the multinational corporation—was started by someone who overcame fear and failure to make their idea a success.

chapter four:
be resourceful without resources

Having no resources, Blake argues, can sometimes be a blessing in disguise. For one thing, if a company has no money in the bank, it cannot possibly lose very much. There's nowhere to go but up. If your "office" is really a garage or the back room in an apartment, you pay no rent for office space. Plus, your employees will feel the excitement of being involved in a start-up. This shared experience of hardship can draw your company together, promote group unity, and keep everyone energized and pointed in the same direction. Having limited resources is not just good for morale. It also creates a culture of creativity and entrepreneurship that will come in handy when the company has more money and resources at its disposal.

DISCUSSION QUESTIONS

1. How can having limited resources actually work to your advantage? What products or services are must-haves when starting a business?

2. What free resources do you have at your disposal that you could use to start a new project or business? Which of your friends or family members could you reach out to for help?

3. What type of challenges do organizations face when they get bigger? As a business begins to scale, how do you keep the "magic" of the start-up phase?

4. On a number of occasions, Blake positioned to potential partners and customers that TOMS was bigger than it actually was. How did he do this? What are the positive qualities that you assume large companies have that smaller companies don't? What advantages do smaller companies have?

5. Starting off as a seat-of-the-pants operation can become part of your brand's story. Can you think of any companies known for their humble beginnings? How does that aspect of their story influence your attitude toward the company?

WORDS INTO ACTION

1. **One man's trash**... Blake writes about Tom Szaky, founder of TerraCycle, a company that turns worm poop into fertilizer, candy wrappers into school supplies, and old fruit-juice containers into backpacks. Take a moment to think of the free or low-cost resources that you have access to. How could you turn trash into treasure?

2. **More money, more problems?** If an investor gave you a million dollars to start a business, how would your approach compare

to just having $1,000 of your own money? What are the advantages and disadvantages of each situation?

3. **Trimming the fat.** Antoine de Saint-Exupéry once said, "Perfection is achieved, not when there is nothing more to add, but when there is nothing left to take away." The next time you enter a business, try to identify three aspects of the business that could be eliminated without diminishing the quality of the product or service being offered.

chapter five: Keep it simple

Simplicity is deep in the TOMS DNA. The *alpargata* has been around for over a century, during which time its design has been refined to as few elements as possible. Just as important is the simplicity of the TOMS business model: "With every pair you purchase, TOMS will give a pair of new shoes to a child in need. One for One."™ "The easier it is for someone to understand who you are and what you stand for," Blake writes, "the easier it will be for that person to spread the word to others."

Simplicity can be difficult to achieve, but a simple product can have an advantage over its competition, even when the competition's product has extra features. The iPod, for example, originally consisted of nothing but a wheel, a button, and a screen—a radical simplicity that has helped it overcome the fact that it lacks, for example, a radio and an easily replaceable battery.

DISCUSSION QUESTIONS

1. Why is simplicity so hard to achieve? What's the difference between achieving simplicity and merely being simplistic?

2. Take a story you know well, such as a fairy tale or a popular movie, and simplify its plot to a few sentences while still retaining what makes it interesting.

3. How is Google different from other search engines like Yahoo! and AOL? Is it possible for a product to be both simple and complex—*at the same time*?

4. The In-N-Out burger chain serves burgers, fries, and sodas—nothing else. How is this a business advantage compared to other fast-food chains like McDonald's or Burger King?

5. The simplicity of the *alpargata* allows TOMS to experiment with its business model in ways that would not be possible if their product were more complicated. Take Style Your Sole parties—how do they depend upon simplicity? How do they in turn increase customers' connection to the brand? What are some products that, due to their complexity, prevent this kind of connection from forming?

WORDS INTO ACTION

1. **Hi, tech!** iPods are simple because they incorporate cutting-edge technologies in an intuitive way. They are easy for beginners to use,

but equally enjoyable for more tech-savvy customers. What are other products or gadgets that seamlessly incorporate technology? What technologies are so new that they have yet to be simplified?

2. **Outsourcing 101.** Tim Ferriss has used the 80/20 rule to radically improve his productivity and time management. How can you apply the 80/20 rule to your own life? What time-consuming or mundane tasks could you outsource to a virtual assistant? What's the most unusual or fun thing that you could delegate?

3. **The elusive obvious.** Jacob Davis made his name solving a simple problem that had gone unnoticed for a long time: People's pants kept falling down. The world is full of problems that are ubiquitous but not serious enough to attract much attention. What are three such challenges that you might be able to solve?

chapter six: **build trust**

DISCUSSION QUESTIONS

1. Plenty of companies have broken the bond of trust with customers and, as a result, suffered losses in revenue or even gone out of business. What are some examples from the past few years? In each case, what assumption about the bond between company and customer was undermined?

2. On the other hand, many companies have made serious mistakes and hardly suffered at all. How did the responses made by

these companies differ from those made by the companies in Question #1?

3. What do you think of Zappos' policy of offering new employees $3,000 to leave their job if they're feeling unsatisfied? If you worked at Zappos, would you take this offer? How does this policy affect company culture for the employees that choose to stay?

4. Trust in the servant-leader model goes both ways—the employer needs to trust the employee, and vice versa. How are the expectations of each group similar? Different?

5. Building trust takes time and dedication; it's not something that you can create by following an exact formula. Think of some of the high-trust relationships that you've experienced—whether at school, work, or in your personal life. What has made these relationships so positive? How are these relationships different than the low-trust environments that you've been in?

WORDS INTO ACTION

1. **You don't know what you've got . . .** You often don't notice a bond of trust until it's broken. What are some basic assumptions that you make about your relationship with your school? Your work? Your local coffee shop? Have you ever felt that your trust has been broken? How did this affect your behavior and feelings moving forward?

2. **Nonprofits 2.0.** Think of a nonprofit organization that you've given money to in the past, or feel a strong connection to. Using

charity: water as an example: How could your selected nonprofit build more trust with you? What would motivate you to give more of your time or money?

3. **Striking a balance.** Can servant leadership be applied to every type of organization, or do you think that some organizations require a more hierarchical and authoritarian leadership style? Could servant leadership be utilized by governments? Professional sports teams? The military?

chapter seven: giving is good business

"Milton Friedman is often quoted as saying that the only social responsibility of business is to increase its profits," Blake writes, "but such thinking is out of date and out of gas." Just as corporate management styles now emphasize networks of trust over hierarchies of power, entrepreneurs have begun to realize that giving not only feels good—it's actually good for business. An obsession with the bottom line can alienate customers and vendors, but if a company includes giving in its business model, it stands to come out ahead by attracting customers who want their purchases to mean something.

DISCUSSION QUESTIONS

1. If TOMS just made canvas shoes, and didn't incorporate giving into its business model, would the company be as successful as it is today? As Blake was bootstrapping to get the company off the

ground, how would things have been different? Would customers still be excited by Style Your Sole parties and One Day Without Shoes?

2. How is being a giving-based business an advantage when it comes to attracting partners? What value did AT&T get from featuring TOMS in a national commercial? What value did TOMS get?

3. How is the business model of FEED Projects similar to that of TOMS? How is it different?

4. TOMS makes shoes and eyewear. FEED Projects makes canvas bags. What other types of companies might be good candidates for incorporating giving into their business models?

5. Can you think of any type of company where incorporating giving might *not* make sense? How could a brick-making company incorporate giving into its business? What about a software company? A coffee shop?

WORDS INTO ACTION

1. **Nonprofit vs. for-profit.** Think of a handful of your favorite nonprofits. Could these organizations do more good as for-profit companies? Are there some instances where being a for-profit business just isn't viable, or where the cause would be better served by a nonprofit?

2. **Finding your story in others.** When is the last time you bought a product or service because you liked the company's mission?

What about the brand's story did you find important or moving? Are there some products or services that you would buy regardless of the company that makes them?

3. *Unconscious consumerism.* As conscious consumerism becomes more widespread, some companies will increasingly pay lip service to being socially and environmentally friendly, without actually being so. Have you experienced any examples of this? As you begin to start something that matters, how can you ensure that authenticity is woven into everything you do?

chapter eight: the final step

Tyler Eltringham was inspired by TOMS to create OneShot, a nonprofit organization dedicated to providing meningitis vaccinations to college students living in university housing; and for every vaccine administered in the United States, OneShot gives a shot to a person in need in the meningitis belt of Africa. Eltringham was still an undergraduate student when he launched OneShot, and had no previous experience in business or entrepreneurship. But he didn't let that stop him. The "final step," Mycoskie explains, is actually the first step: You will never be fully prepared, but you have to start something anyway. You have to get moving!

DISCUSSION QUESTIONS

1. Knowledge can be a powerful tool, but it can also paralyze you into inaction. When you're first getting started, how can you go about the research phase without getting overwhelmed? What information is indispensable when starting a new business or project?

2. Blake writes, "Someone once told me the key to staying healthy was tying his shoes." Why is this good advice for someone starting a business venture? What are some examples of "tying your shoes" in business?

3. What are some of the challenges facing a start-up like One-Shot? How does OneShot use giving to connect its philanthropic and business elements? How does this connection make OneShot's story resonate?

4. How was Tyler resourceful without resources in creating One-Shot? In what ways is being a college student an advantage when starting a new project or business? What free resources are available to students?

5. The first step is often the hardest to take because it involves moving into unfamiliar territory. But the truth is that the challenges that occur later in an endeavor are often more difficult to overcome, but they don't feel nearly as hard. Why is this?

WORDS INTO ACTION

1. **Is ignorance bliss?** Think about a big project, school assignment, or hobby that you've worked on in the past and the challenges that you faced along the way. Would knowing about those problems ahead of time have affected your decision to undertake the project? Would you have been scared off? Was it better not to know about them?

2. **It's good to have friends.** Think about all of the people in your life—your friends, family, and members of your community. As you're thinking about starting something that matters, who are five people who you could reach out to for advice? How could each of these people help you?

3. **Carpe diem.** Now that you've finished *Start Something That Matters*, how will you seize the day? Are you interested in starting a business, nonprofit, or just making a big change in your life? How will you get your project off the ground?

about the author

In 2006, Blake Mycoskie founded TOMS Shoes, the company that would match every pair purchased with a new pair given to a child in need. One for One. In September 2010, Blake returned to Argentina, where he was first inspired to start TOMS, to celebrate the one millionth pair of new shoes given to a child in need.

After five amazing years of giving shoes, Blake was ready to address another need: vision. On June 7, 2011, TOMS debuted One for One Eyewear, which provides eye treatment, prescription glasses, or eye surgery for every pair purchased.

Former President Bill Clinton has introduced Blake as "one of the most interesting entrepreneurs [he has] ever met." And Bill Gates featured Blake and TOMS Shoes in his *Time* magazine article, "How to Fix Capitalism."

Blake is an avid reader and traveler. A favorite quote of his by Gandhi: "Be the change you want to see in the world."